Companion to
THE TRIATHLETE'S TRAINING BIBLE

2nd edition

Joe Friel

Boulder, Colorado

1830 55th Street
Boulder, Colorado 80301-2700 USA
303/440-0601 · Fax 303/444-6788 · E-mail velopress@competitorgroup.com

Distributed in the United States and Canada by Publishers Group West

Library of Congress Cataloging-in-Publication Data
Friel, Joe.
    A companion to the Triathlete's training bible / Joe Friel.—2nd ed.
        p. cm.
    SBN 978-1-934030-34-9 (alk. paper)
    1. Triathlon—Training. I. Title. II. Title: Triathlete's training bible.
GV1060.73.F734   2009
796.42'57—dc22

                            2009016156

For information on purchasing VeloPress books, please call 800/234-8356
or visit www.velopress.com.

Cover design by xxx
Interior design and composition by Erin Johnson

11 10 09 / 10 9 8 7 6 5 4 3 2 1

Contents

Preface   v

Acknowledgments   vii

1   Smart Training   1

2   Attitude   7

3   The Science of Training   13

4   Intensity   19

5   Assessing Fitness   35

6   Building Fitness   41

7   Planning a Year   45

8   Planning a Week   51

9   Planning to Race   59

10   Racing   65

11   Recovery   73

12   Skills   79

13   Muscles   93

14   Unique Needs   103

15   The Training Diary   105

16   Fuel   109

About the Author   116

Preface to the Companion

It's been almost 12 years since I wrote *The Triathlete's Training Bible*. During that period a lot has changed, prompting me to revisit the book. Most of the changes made were additions, so the third edition grew considerably larger, just as the sport has grown in the past twelve years. When I sat down to write *The Triathlete's Training Bible* in 1997, the USA Triathlon Federation had 16,212 licensed members. The sport was still in its infancy. When I started this revision in 2007, the USAT had more than 100,000 members.

The sport has grown in a way none of us who were there in the early days could ever have imagined. It is now mainstream. When I first wrote *The Triathlete's Training Bible*, I knew of only five other books on the topic. Now major bookstores have a section on their shelves just for triathlon. Fictional characters on television shows are triathletes. Celebrities do triathlons. When you tell someone you ride a bike, the first thing they ask is whether you're a triathlete. When your neighbors see you heading out for your daily bike and run, they no longer think you're a wacko; they know you're a triathlete. Web sites devoted to triathlon were practically nonexistent 12 years ago. Now there are thousands. What a remarkable change we've experienced in such a short time.

This growth has caused the sport of triathlon to change in other ways as well. Twelve years ago the average triathlete was more knowledgeable about current trends in training, nutrition, equipment, and racing. Of course, at the time there was a lot less information out there to be aware of. In the past 12 years there has been an explosion not only of training information but also of training technology. Power meters were pretty much unheard of in 1997, and GPS training devices and accelerometers existed only in our imaginations.

Our knowledge of every aspect of training has grown. Physiology and nutrition have led the way, with sports psychology lagging just a bit behind. As a result, how we should train and eat are much better-defined than in

1997. But I'm afraid a result of this explosion of information and technology is that triathletes are more confused than ever. That's why I felt a need to revise *The Triathlete's Training Bible.*

I've also grown as a coach in the past 12 years. Back then I could keep up with almost every new development that came down the pike—wheels, running shoes, sports nutritional products, goggles, wetsuits, bike frames, skill techniques, races, Web sites, books, and on and on. Now I find that I have to focus my attention on just a few of these, the ones I find to be most important. As a result, I now know a great deal more about fewer things. I've tried to describe these things in the latest edition.

Although every chapter of the third edition of *The Triathlete's Training Bible* features new material, the most significant additions have been in the chapters devoted to the intensity of training (Chapter 4), skills (Chapter 12), strength (Chapter 13), and nutrition (Chapter 16). This Companion volume includes all of the additions to make it easy for you to find what is new if you own and have already read the second edition. There are always edits or clarifications that seem to be necessary when revising a book, but these minor changes will not be included in the Companion. You can also go to my Web site—http://trainingbible.com—for ongoing updates to many of the concepts found here.

You can use the cross-references provided to refresh your memory regarding more complicated concepts. You'll find page numbers cited in the margins of the text.

TRIATHLETE'S
TRAINING BIBLE
2nd ed.

See p. "x"

As always, I hope my book proves helpful to you in pursuit of the triathlon lifestyle. If it does (or even if it doesn't), feel free to e-mail me at jfriel@ trainingbible.com. I attend many races throughout the season and would enjoy talking with you about your triathlon experience. Hearing from those who benefit from my books is always a great pleasure and gives meaning to what is otherwise a solitary and tedious activity.

I wish you all the best for your training and racing!

Joe Friel
Boulder, Colorado

Acknowledgments

I am indebted, as always, to the triathletes who have read *The Triathlete's Training Bible* and given me their suggestions for making it a more useful tool. The idea for this Companion to the second edition came from many such athletes who commented that they did not want to buy a third edition and then search it for the changes.

I also want to thank the staff at VeloPress, my publisher, who continue to support my ideas for books and create products that get better every year. Special thanks go to Renee Jardine, associate publisher, for championing my idea for this format and for continuing to support my writing projects. Thanks also to Dave Trendler, marketing manager, for getting the word out whenever I give a Training Bible–based talk.

Three athletes I have coached agreed to allow me to use their experiences in this book: Ryan Bolton, Justin Daerr, and Marlene Zuhl. Thank you.

Nate Koch, P.T., A.T.C., director of rehabilitation at Endurance Rehabilitation in Scottsdale, Arizona, who assesses all of my coaching clients, reviewed the physical assessment section in Chapter 5 and offered suggestions. Thanks, Nate.

And, of course, thanks to my loving wife, Joyce, who after 41 years of marriage continues to support my passion for sports science by putting up with my 4 a.m. writing sessions and late evenings at the computer. Thanks, sweetheart.

1: Smart Training

Good training needs to be systematic and consistent. Both goals can be reinforced when you take the time to develop a successful training philosophy. If you want to be a better triathlete, you must have a firm grasp on what makes people successful in any endeavor.

10 LESSONS FOR SMARTER TRAINING

I was once asked to speak about the most important lessons I had learned in nearly three decades of coaching. It was a good exercise, as it ultimately helped me to summarize my coaching philosophy and highlight the key points. As I prepared my list, it became apparent that the essential lessons of smart training were quite basic. Here is a list of what I think are the ten most important lessons for success as a triathlete.

Lesson 1: Have a clear goal. Most athletes think they have goals. Few really do. What most call goals are actually wishes. They are vague desires for grand achievements that are poorly defined. These also often include the word "faster." When first starting a coaching program for an athlete, I help him or her turn these wishes into goals by asking questions such as How much? When? Where? Is this goal a good stretch for you? Is it realistic? Another good question to ask in order to better define one's goals is How will you know if this season was successful? We do talk about dreams when I ask, What is the greatest accomplishment you'd like to achieve as a triathlete? Long-term dreams can eventually become goals. Knowing precisely what you want is critical to success in triathlon just as it is in life. Goal setting is discussed in greater detail in Chapter 7.

Lesson 2: Determine what stands between you and your goal. A good goal will stretch your limits. Pushing yourself to reach that goal obviously requires that you improve some aspect of yourself, and you need to identify whatever that "something" is. Instead of training randomly by doing what you've done in the past, what your training partners want to do, or the workouts some pro does, you should isolate and improve the quality you are lacking. This is kind of an engineer's way of looking at training, but it works. I call it "fixing the limiters." You'll find more on this in Chapter 6.

Lesson 3: Planning is necessary to achieve big goals. This may sound boring, but planning is at the heart of training, especially when your goals are big ones. I know you may have heard good athletes say that they don't plan and do quite well anyway. I'd wager they really are following a plan, but it's not in writing. The plan is in their heads. Good athletes don't become good by training randomly, and you won't either. *The Triathlete's Training Bible* is essentially about planning. Chapter 7 provides the details on how to map out a seasonal plan, Chapter 8 covers race-week planning, and Chapter 9 discusses race-day planning.

Lesson 4: Measure progress toward your goals. There's nothing worse than thinking you are making good progress toward achieving your goal and later finding out on race day that you are not physically ready. Had you known earlier that you weren't improving as expected in some aspect of fitness, you might have had time to correct it by changing your training. There are many ways to assess fitness progress. Chapter 5 addresses some of these.

Lesson 5: Do the least amount of training necessary to achieve your goal. This training philosophy, though noted above, is worth repeating. When I was a much younger athlete, I thought my success depended on training as much as possible. That approach led to frequent injury, overtraining, illness, and burnout. It took me many years to figure out what I should be doing—only the training that was necessary to achieve my goals. Once I cut out the excessive stuff, I got better as an athlete. This book will return again and again to the theme of identifying what is important and then doing only that.

Lesson 6: Mental fitness is as important as physical fitness. Chapter 2 discusses mental toughness. I believe the key mental skill is confidence. Of all the factors I consider when talking to the athletes I coach, this is the most important. What I look for in athletes is a quiet, "can-do" attitude. This is the common denominator for all of the best athletes I have known. A great deal of self-doubt is a sure sign of someone who is incapable of achieving high goals regardless of physical ability.

Lesson 7: Skill is critical to athletic success. In endurance sports, with the possible exception of swimming, athletes tend to downplay or even disregard technique. Most athletes, including elites, have lots of room for improvement in their sport-specific skills. As skills improve, less energy is wasted, which means you can go faster for the same effort. Your movements are more economical. Skills and economy are discussed in Chapter 12.

Lesson 8: Train for the unique demands of the goal race. Every race is unique. The principal factor is race distance, such as sprint or Ironman distance. Beyond this are other, less obvious factors: A course may be over hilly, rolling, or flat terrain; the water may be rough or calm; there are wetsuit and non-wetsuit swims, hot and cold temperatures, courses with lots of turns or very few turns, off-road and road courses, morning and afternoon start times, races in which you will use a disk wheel and those in which you will not, and a multitude of other variables. Your training, as you get closer to race day, should take on more and more of the unique characteristics of the race you are preparing for. In Chapter 10, you will learn how to write a race plan that takes key variables into consideration: Learn to take charge of the factors you can control, and learn how to deal with those you can't.

> Training is composed of two elements: hard work and recovery. One without the other makes for an ineffective program.

Lesson 9: Recovery is just as important as hard workouts. Training is composed of two elements: hard work and recovery. One without the other makes for an ineffective program. I've found that most triathletes have no problem at all with the hard work part. In fact, they seem to thrive on it. Where most need help is with recovery. Left to their own devices, most triathletes will work too hard and rest too little. And since it is during rest that the body adapts and becomes fitter, training overly hard and resting too little is counterproductive. Chapter 11 takes a closer look at the details of recovery.

Lesson 10: Focus your lifestyle on success. The bigger your triathlon goals are relative to your abilities, the more things in your life that must be focused on achieving your goals. If your goal is to complete a sprint-distance race, you can afford to be a bit sloppy with nutrition, sleep, stress, training partners, friends, stretching, equipment, workout analysis, and strength work and still do well. But if your goal is to win a national championship or qualify for Ironman Hawaii®, you will need to get everything in your life pointed at triathlon success. Since the people who ask me to coach them are aiming for big goals, I spend a lot of time helping them focus their lifestyles on success. Chapters 13 through 16 address most of these issues.

One last bit of advice. Have fun. This may seem obvious, but some athletes are so focused on achieving the right numbers in their logs that they've forgotten why they got involved in the sport in the first place. They've taken the fun out of it. Many of the pros I talk to are amazed at how much training time age groupers do on top of working 50 to 60 hours per week, raising a couple of kids, getting them to soccer practice, taking care of the landscaping, doing volunteer work, and myriad other responsibilities. By comparison, the pros have it easy; they just train 30 to 40 hours per week with a few naps sprinkled in. But they also tell me that if it ever stops being fun, they will quit racing and get a real job. Fun is the reason each of us participates in triathlon. Smile more. Frown less.

7 TRAINING MISTAKES (NEARLY) EVERYONE MAKES

It's amazing how often I see the same mistakes made over and over by athletes. In fact, I have found seven mistakes that everyone, from novice to experienced pro, makes at least once each season. You will notice that each of these mistakes reinforces the importance of the lessons covered earlier.

Mistake 1: No direction. Almost every athlete has goals, but there are two problems with the goals most set. The typical athlete makes "I want to get better" goals that are so vague there is no way to know if progress is being made. That leads to the second problem: About the time the hard training or racing begins, the goals are forgotten. The athlete becomes so absorbed in preparing for the next race that he or she becomes myopic about training. It's like the old saying, "They can't see the forest for the trees."

Mistake 2: No priorities. The second most common mistake is to treat every race as critical. It's easy to make this mistake, especially if you're doing a series of races that all count toward final standings. The problem with not having priorities is that there is never an opportunity to come to a true peak. That means you never fully realize what you're capable of doing in a race, and that means permanent mediocrity.

Training Safety

Training for endurance sports involves taking risks. Some of the risks you take may even be life-threatening, but you can minimize them by taking certain precautions.

Cycling typically carries the greatest risk of the three sports because of the reliance on the bicycle and because of the distances a triathlete must ride on the open road in training. To minimize the danger, avoid heavily trafficked areas whenever possible, and always wear a helmet. Ride only with safe groups, not with people who run stop signs, ride in between traffic, or generally ignore traffic laws. Never take undue risks on steep descents while riding. And before every ride, test your brakes, check the quick releases to make sure they are tight, examine the tires to see if they have any cuts or show signs of too much wear, and tighten any loose bolts.

Swimming can also be risky, particularly if you train in open water. Never swim in open water alone. Always swim with a partner, and ideally, with a kayak "spotter." Kayakers often volunteer for organized group training swims in open water. Similarly, if there is no lifeguard present for a pool swim, make sure you train with a partner.

Running on open roads requires safety precautions similar to those you would take in cycling. Avoid heavily trafficked roads. If you run within an hour of dawn or dusk, wear reflective material. Be aware of whether the sun will be in drivers' eyes, making it difficult for them to see you. As for which side of the road to run on, it is your choice—there are no laws saying you must run on one side or the other. (This is a contrast to cycling, as cyclists must ride in the direction of traffic, as close as practicable to the right.) I prefer to run against traffic so I can see what's coming toward me, but if you do so, be aware of drivers about to turn onto the road you are on, because they may not be looking in your direction when they enter the intersection. Finally, run only with safe groups who respect traffic laws.

Also, whether you are swimming, cycling, or running, if you experience any unusual physical conditions, such as chest pain, radiating arm or neck pain, an unusually high or erratic heart rate, joint soreness, back pain, unusual muscle or tendon discomfort, or blood in the urine, be sure to inform your doctor right away. Such conditions should also cause you to stop the workout immediately. Let's have a safe and successful season.

Mistake 3: Training the wrong stuff. What stands between you and success? Most athletes have a pretty good idea, but they don't work hard enough at correcting the weakness. It's like the old saying, "A chain is only as strong as its weakest link." If your weak link is climbing hills on the bike and the season's most important race is on a hilly bike course, you'd better be doing a lot to climb better. Paying lip service to climbing while spending a lot of time and energy running, which you may enjoy more, won't do much to produce good race results. The weak link is still weak.

Mistake 4: Doing intervals too soon. I've never figured out why athletes are so eager to start intervals. I see athletes who don't have a race until May doing gut-busting intervals in December. What do they hope to accomplish? I hope you're not making this mistake, but there's a good chance you are.

Mistake 5: Not enough rest. This is probably the most common mistake; it's made by nearly everyone who is even a little bit serious about training. I suspect it's so common because of the personality traits of those who are successful in sport. They learned at an early age that hard work produces results. So what do they do when things are going well? They work harder. How about when things aren't going well? They work harder. They see hard work as the solution to all problems. This inevitably leads to overtraining (see mistake 6).

Mistake 6: Ignoring fatigue. Why do we all believe that we're Superman or Superwoman? After all, everyone understands that too much training and too little rest, if continued long enough, result in overtraining. It certainly makes sense. Yet when the signs of overtraining appear, we ignore them and continue as if they're minor hindrances. "Overtraining can't happen to me" is the general belief.

Mistake 7: Not tapering for big races. Either athletes don't know how to taper for important races, or they're afraid of losing fitness by backing off. Every year at Ironman Hawaii® I see athletes doing excessively long workouts the week of the race. Don't they understand that race-week rest is what will produce their best race on Saturday? I'll never understand this one.

Preventing these mistakes is essentially what a coach does for you. Coaches know that if they can just keep an athlete out of his or her own way, the race results will take care of themselves. It's time to become a better self-coach by eliminating such mistakes. I'd like to help you do that.

2: Attitude

We all know that success in triathlon begins with a passion for the sport. When you love the swimming, cycling, and running, the demands of training are much easier to accommodate. Commitment, however, usually entails some kind of sacrifice. Even if you love triathlon, if you stick with the sport long enough, it will eventually require that you reach beyond what is easy or natural for you to accomplish in order to achieve the next level of performance. It will test your limits—both your athletic abilities and your mind. It promises to be an exhilarating experience.

MENTAL TOUGHNESS

Why are Lance Armstrong, Tiger Woods, and Michael Jordan often referred to as the greatest of all time in their respective sports? Is it due to genetics or opportunity? To nature or nurture? Are they "naturals" who were destined to succeed once they had the chance to appear on the playing field?

These are hard questions to answer because it's difficult to separate innate ability from hard work. But one thing we can certainly see in these three exemplary athletes is their dedication to improvement. Armstrong was well-known for daily six-hour rides, repeated practice on key routes of the Tour de France, and weighing every bite of food that went into his mouth.

After Woods won the 1997 Masters Tournament by a record 12 strokes over second place, he set about improving his swing so he could be even better. After winning the four major tournaments on the PGA Tour in succession, the only man ever to do so, he again went back to work on improving his swing. And he has single-handedly changed the work ethic among pro golfers.

Michael Jordan was cut from his junior high school basketball team, which made him determined to prove himself. Never one to rest on his laurels, Jordan developed a reputation even at the pro level for his dedication to improvement, often staying after practice to work on his "weaknesses."

It would appear that hard work was a major component in the success of each of these athletes. But was it the main reason for their success? Recent research seems to indicate that it was. This research goes even further by suggesting that it takes ten years of focused work on one's sport to reach the threshold of greatness. That was certainly true with Armstrong, Woods, and Jordan. Lance Armstrong won the Iron Kids Triathlon at age 13 and nine years later was crowned the world road champion in cycling. At age 8, Woods took his first big win in the Optimist International Junior Championship, which he went on to win five more times. His victory at the 1997 Masters came at age 21, 13 years later. After being cut from the basketball team, Jordan began to train and practice

Being mentally tough is what eventually produces high-level performance in athletes once they have achieved their physiological peak.

rigorously and at age 16 was the leading scorer on his high school team. Nine years later, as a member of the Chicago Bulls, he was named the most valuable player in the NBA.

As a coach for three decades, I've seen essentially the same thing—athletes improve physiologically for about seven years. They continue to improve their race performances for at least another three years because they apply their experience, knowing what it takes in training, racing, and lifestyle to succeed. This timeline holds true regardless of the age at which an athlete starts training and competing.

I believe that the key to all of this hard work is more mental than physical. Being mentally tough, like triathletes in the early days of the sport, is what eventually produces high-level performance in athletes once they have achieved their physiological peak. What does it take to be mentally tough? There are four qualities I look for in athletes who say they want to perform at the highest levels: a desire to succeed, self-discipline, an attitude of believing in themselves, and patience (or perseverance). To evaluate whether you possess these qualities, ask yourself the questions that I ask athletes, which are included below.

Desire to Succeed

- Can you train alone, or do you need to be with others to motivate you to complete hard sessions?
- Do you find a way to work out regardless of environmental conditions such as rain, snow, wind, heat, darkness, or other potential training interruptions?

I find that athletes who regularly train alone tend to have higher levels of mental toughness and a great desire to succeed. The same holds for those who train in the rain and cold, or who find a way to regularly train despite busy work schedules and family commitments.

Discipline

- Do you shape your training and lifestyle to fit your goals?
- How important to you are nutrition, sleep, periodization, goal setting, physical skills, attitude, health, and strength?
- Do your family and friends support you and your goals?

There are athletes who fit training into their lives as much as possible, and those for whom the daily workout is paramount and nearly everything else is secondary. I look for athletes who make workouts, diet, and rest a regular and reliable part of daily life. When those athletes are surrounded by a good support network, they're most likely to stick with a training program.

Belief in Self

- Do you go into a race with a success plan?
- Do you really believe you can succeed even when the conditions are not favorable?
- When it comes to racing, which do you think more about—the controllable variables or the uncontrollable variables?
- Do you accept occasional setbacks as necessary steps on the way to success, or as signs you simply can't do it?
- Do you believe you can, or question whether you can?

I have seen gifted athletes who didn't believe in their own potential, and I've seen those athletes defeated by physically weaker but mentally tougher competitors. If you don't truly believe that you can improve and win, it will be difficult for a coach to convince you otherwise.

Patience and Perseverance

- Are you in this for the long term?
- Do you need immediate success, or can you postpone it until the time is right, even if that is years in the future?
- Do you ever skip training for days or even weeks at a time and then try to get into shape quickly?

As discussed earlier, athletes continue to improve for about ten years, no matter what age they start training. Training to win is a long-term commitment that may have periods of seemingly no progress. Athletes need the patience to work steadily through those periods, knowing that improvement will come later.

My experience has been that if any one of these mental toughness qualities is lacking, the athlete will not achieve his or her lofty career goals. Few athletes have high levels of all these qualities. I've only coached one athlete who I felt had exceptional overall mental toughness. He became a Team USA Olympian, and the story of how he did it is a great illustration of how mental toughness can give you a significant advantage.

CASE STUDY IN MENTAL TOUGHNESS

On the evening of May 20, 2000, Ryan Bolton and I went for a walk in the dark on a golf course near where we were staying in Fort Worth, Texas. The next day would be the U.S. Triathlon Olympic Trials for men. We had been focusing on this day for more than three years. The first two American finishers would qualify for the games in Sydney, Australia—the first time triathlon would be an Olympic sport.

As we walked, we talked about the various scenarios that could unfold the next day and how Ryan should respond to each. We had discussed these possible situations before, but with the big exam tomorrow this was our last chance to review them. We were both a bit nervous but didn't let it show.

Ryan was one of the fastest runners among elite American triathletes. He had been an All American runner at the University of Wyoming and had broken 30 minutes for 10,000 meters. But even though he had those credentials, I told him as we walked that if he came off the bike more than 90 seconds behind the leaders, it would all be over. He wouldn't be able to make up any more time than that on an elite field, so he had to be close by T2 should something go wrong on the swim or bike.

The next day, things did go wrong. Our worst possible scenario occurred: Ryan had a poor swim, getting slightly off-course, and came out of the water near the tail end of the field. There were three Americans along with two Aussies already in transition with a small gap before the remainder of the field and Ryan bringing up the rear. Foreign athletes were allowed to compete for prize money that day but of course could not qualify for Team USA. One of the three Americans leading the race was Hunter Kemper, who had already qualified for the Olympic team. Thus, Ryan had to catch one of the other two Americans to make the team.

Out on the bike course there were three distinct groups. The five leaders worked well together and began to open the gap between them and the large chase group. Ryan and a Brit brought up the tail end. But they worked well together (drafting is allowed in Olympic triathlon) and soon caught back up with the peloton. Ryan's instructions now were to get this chase group organized and to reel in the leaders. But the riders wouldn't cooperate, with each athlete wanting someone else to do the hard work. So the leaders disappeared up the road, and the gap kept growing.

By the time Ryan's group hit T2, the leaders had a 2-minute, 15-second lead. As Ryan came out of transition to start the 10 km run, I yelled, "Two fifteen" at him. He knew what that meant. I was saying, *You can't do it now*, as we had discussed the night before. I was disheartened, but Ryan had fire in his eyes.

I had spotters on the course with walkie-talkies who were reporting time gaps to me. Incredibly, Ryan was closing the gap at a remarkable rate. As he completed the first lap and ran by me again I could see that he was on a mission. He was not going to give up, and he had me believing. He had to catch the third American runner, Doug Friman, to qualify. Doug had only about 75 seconds on him with two laps to go. I yelled, "Seventy-five."

The spotters reported that Ryan was still closing in as he went by each of them on the next lap. Starting the final lap, Ryan caught Doug right in front of me. Incredibly, he had made up 2 minutes and 15 seconds in just over 6 km and was in position to qualify for the Olympics if he held that place. Now I was concerned about the heat. It had been 90 degrees at start time with high humidity. The previous day the leader of the women's race, Barb Lindquist, had succumbed to the heat on the second lap of the run and dropped out. So I shouted at Ryan, "Slow down!" But he would have none of that. He wanted to catch the next American. There was no holding him back.

As he crossed the finish line in third place we hugged and shouted. He had done it! Later, after things settled down, I asked him what had gone through his mind when I had yelled that he was trailing by more than 2 minutes at the start of the run. After all, he could easily have given up and resigned himself to being an "also-ran" that day. The coach had said 90 seconds was all the room he had. "I just knew I could do it," he said.

That day was one of the finest examples of mental toughness I had ever seen in an athlete I coached. Ryan went on to be a tremendous Ironman-distance triathlete after the Olympics. And I never again questioned his mental toughness.

Mental toughness is perhaps where the nurturing part of the success equation is most evident. Some athletes seem to have internalized these qualities at an early age. Others have not. What makes the difference? It is probably hundreds of seemingly insignificant interactions that take place on a daily basis from birth through the formative years, experiences that we don't exactly know how to identify or instill.

Perhaps the best thing you could do to improve your mental toughness is to work with a sports psychologist much the same as you would work with a coach. Sports psychology is a rapidly growing field, and it is becoming increasingly common for athletes at all competitive levels to seek the services of such professionals.

3: The Science of Training

Science can help us understand certain training principles, but it is not a fail-safe method of approaching your training. Studies in a laboratory do not factor in all of the variables that may affect an individual athlete's training and performance, namely yours. You will need to make adjustments to your method to take into account your experience over multiple seasons of training and racing as well as your changing goals from one race to the next.

PEAKING

Coming to a fitness peak at just the right times in the season is the ultimate reason for training. Creating that moment when racing seems effortless makes months of hard work and sweat worthwhile. Yet few athletes ever experience such a fitness high. Even fewer know how to create it.

Most multisport athletes believe that peaking is as simple as reducing the workload for a few days before a big race. There's more to it than that. In fact, such a "taper" will not produce a true fitness peak: The athlete is unlikely to be rested, let alone near the apex of his or her potential.

When a true peak comes about, you will experience several physical changes that combine to create a performance that borders on astonishing. These changes include increased leg power, reduced lactic acid production, increased blood volume, greater red blood cell concentration, and increased fuel storage. Top these physical transformations with sharper mental skills such as concentration, confidence, and motivation, and you are truly in top race form. All of this, and no illegal drugs are needed.

There are three elements of physical preparation to balance in the last two to three weeks before your highest-priority races—fatigue, fitness, and form. Fatigue is a measure of workload. If intensity or volume has recently been high, then fatigue will be elevated.

But when fatigue is high, fitness will also be high. High-intensity and long-duration training produce fatigue and fitness simultaneously—hard workouts make you tired but also make you more fit. Sadly, fatigue increases

Anatomy of a Peak

For perfect race readiness at the right time, you need to mix two key elements—intensity and rest. Here's how: Starting two to three weeks before your most important race, do a short, race-intensity workout that simulates the conditions of the race every third or fourth day. Gradually make these workouts shorter as you progress through the peaking period, so that your weekly volume is dropping and you get more rest.

Volume should drop rather rapidly. To maintain fitness, your intensity must be *at least* heart rate zone 3 (see Chapter 4) or moderately hard. The two or three days of low-intensity, low-duration workouts between these race simulations are the key to erasing fatigue and elevating form. They should also get shorter as peaking progresses.

The week of the race is the time to emphasize rest but still maintain a degree of intensity. Put the long workouts on hold and instead do three or four workouts in which you complete several 90-second intervals at race intensity or at least heart rate zone 3, with 3-minute recoveries. Five days before the race, do five of these 90-second efforts. Four days before, do four times 90 seconds. This pattern continues throughout the week.

The easiest day of race week should be two days before the race. This is usually best as a day off, but for the high-volume athlete it may be a short and easy ride or swim. The day before should also include some race-like intensity within a very brief session—for example, a 15-minute swim followed later in the morning by a combination workout including a 30-minute bike ride and a 15-minute run. Include a few short efforts at race intensity or higher. You should feel rested, strong, and ready to race!

more rapidly than fitness, so three hard workouts in three days will produce a lot of fatigue but only a tiny increase in fitness. Fitness is best measured in weeks, whereas fatigue is usually measured in days.

Form, which measures how rested you are, is also one of the key elements during the peaking process. You can have high form—that is, be well rested (have low fatigue)—without high fitness. In other words, fitness can be low from too much rest. That's not a good thing when you are trying to peak for a race. It is a bit of a balancing act to reduce fatigue, maintain fitness (or allow only a slight decrease), and increase form so that you are peaked and ready to race.

Coming to a fitness peak at just the right times in the season is the ultimate reason for training. Creating that moment when racing seems effortless makes months of hard work and sweat worthwhile.

This use of the word "form" comes from late-nineteenth-century British horse racing when bettors would review a page of previous race results—a form—of the horses entered in a race. A horse was said to be "on form" when racing well.

In triathlon, the peaking process is complicated further by the variety of sports. For example, running requires a longer taper than cycling does, but the cycling taper should be longer than the swimming taper. There are other elements to consider, such as the length of the race (long races require long tapers), how fit you are (high fitness requires long tapers), how easily injured you are (injury-prone athletes need longer tapers), and how old you are (older athletes need longer tapers).

PERIODIZATION

If you've been using *The Triathlete's Training Bible*, you are no stranger to the concept of periodization. In Chapter 3 of my book I explained how periodization works. If you've put it into practice in your own training, your year is divided into periods and in each period you focus on improving a specific aspect of your fitness while maintaining the gains made in previous periods. Periodization has become such a common method for serious athletes in all sports that it is often mistakenly referred to as a necessary principle of training. Even though it is quite effective in producing fitness peaks at the right times while preventing overtraining and burnout, it is not the only path to

TRIATHLETE'S
TRAINING BIBLE
2nd ed.

*See pp. 27–29
for more on
Periodization*

excellence. Training by following the concepts of periodization is, however, the most likely way known today to achieve athletic success.

Periodization Alternatives

Figure 1 illustrates what is known as "linear" or "classic" periodization. With this model you start the season in the Base period, focusing primarily on the volume of training by doing long and frequent workouts at a low intensity. This creates a high level of aerobic endurance fitness. Then in the Build period you decrease volume by doing long sessions less frequently while increasing the intensity of your training. This improves muscular endurance and anaerobic endurance (described in detail in Chapter 6). All of the training suggestions in this book are based on this linear periodization model. While it is the easiest to understand and the most common way of organizing the training season for endurance athletes, it is not the only model. Two others that are common in triathlon are "undulating" periodization and "reverse linear" periodization.

FIGURE 1: Linear (Classic) Periodization

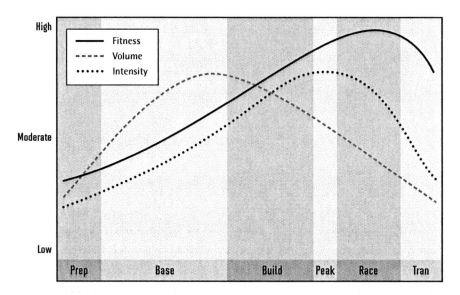

Undulating Periodization

Figure 2 shows how this model works. Essentially, volume and intensity rise and fall alternately as the season progresses. For example, an athlete could pair high-volume biking with high-intensity running one week, and then do high-volume running and high-intensity biking the next. The variety can help to maintain motivation. Research has shown that weightlifters using this model make significant improvements in strength performance. Research is lacking for endurance sports, however.

FIGURE 2: Undulating Periodization

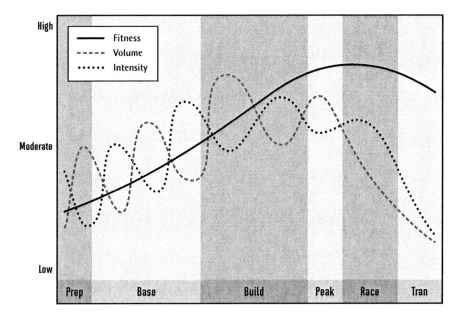

Reverse Linear Periodization

Figure 3 shows just the reverse of the model shown in Figure 1—intensity is high in the Base period, and volume reaches a high point in the Build period. This model works best with long-course triathletes. High intensity and low volume early in the season boost aerobic capacity (VO_2max), and lower-intensity, longer workouts later on develop aerobic endurance. This has the potential to bring you into excellent fitness for long events such as Ironman- and half-Ironman-distance races. It may not be as effective for shorter races.

FIGURE 3: Reverse Linear Periodization

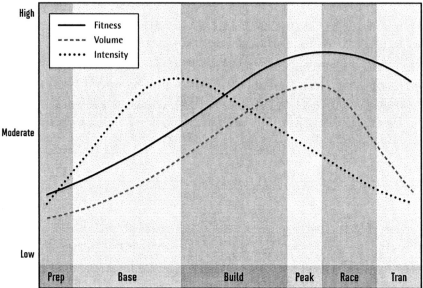

The periodization platform you choose should be one that you understand and are committed to. Linear periodization is generally the easiest model to understand and put into place, and it is still the model used by most athletes around the world, regardless of their levels of performance. I've found the other models to have very little established research behind them, and training guidelines are therefore lacking. Trying to create and follow such a plan would involve a lot of trial and error and would likely result in uneven performances. With linear periodization, you can be confident that you are following a well-researched, proven plan for success.

4: Intensity

I n this chapter I discuss how to fight fatigue and how to intelligently use intensity in your training. In understanding intensity, it is important to have a firm grasp of the concepts of lactate threshold and aerobic threshold.

AEROBIC VERSUS LACTATE THRESHOLD

Aerobic threshold is a critical threshold for triathletes racing at all distances, but especially at Ironman distance. It occurs at a much lower intensity than lactate threshold does. Because lactate threshold occurs at a higher intensity level, it is more important for the triathletes who are competing at more moderate distances, such as Olympic- and sprint-distance races.

TRIATHLETE'S TRAINING BIBLE
2nd ed.

See pp. 33–34 for more on Lactate Threshold

Aerobic threshold is important for the Ironman athlete because such a long-distance event is raced at about this intensity, particularly for the athlete who finishes roughly in the range of 10 to 13 hours. Ironman triathletes finishing faster than about 10 hours will race well above aerobic threshold, and those taking more than about 13 hours will stay below the aerobic threshold throughout the event.

You will recall that the lactate threshold is marked by the accumulation of lactic acid in the body. One way to determine your lactate threshold is to measure your lactate production in a lab or clinic (see *Companion* Chapter 5). Your aerobic threshold is less precisely measured but is physiologically marked by a slight increase in the depth of breathing accompanied by a sense of moderate-effort intensity.

The Role of Hydrogen Ions in Lactate Threshold

To produce energy for movement, the muscles primarily use fat and carbohydrate for fuel. When carbohydrate—the sugar-based fuel source—breaks down, lactic acid is produced in the muscles. As this lactic acid seeps out of the muscle cell and into the blood and surrounding body fluids, hydrogen ions are released, and the resulting sale is called lactate. The amount of hydrogen ions and lactate increases as the intensity of the exercise increases. At low levels of production, the body efficiently removes and recycles them. Even now, hydrogen ions and lactate are appearing in your blood and being removed. Lactate threshold is that point in exertion when the production of the hydrogen ions and lactate is too rapid for the body to keep up. The hydrogen ions are the real concern, a slight variation on previous thought, but by measuring lactate you can find out how much hydrogen is present. Hydrogen ions interfere with energy production and muscular contractions, ultimately causing fatigue. By performing short, high-intensity efforts followed by long recoveries, you can improve your body's ability to remove the hydrogen ions, improving your lactate threshold.

In terms of heart rate, aerobic threshold occurs at the lower end of what I call zone 2. But your heart rate at aerobic threshold will probably vary from one sport to another according to how fit you are for each. For example, if you are a strong cyclist with years of riding behind you, your aerobic threshold may be well into the zone 2 heart rate. But if you've just started swimming seriously, that threshold may be somewhere in zone 1.

Your aerobic threshold in a given sport will also vary from day to day based on how well rested you are. When you are fresh, your aerobic threshold will be found at a higher intensity than when you are fatigued. Because aerobic threshold is something of a moving target, it can be easy to push past it while working out by merely watching your heart rate zones, paying little attention to signs of fatigue. To truly stay below or at your aerobic threshold, your perceived effort is just as important as watching your heart rate monitor (the same is true with lactate threshold, but the intensity there is so great that fatigue will usually keep you from overdoing it). We will take a closer look at how to determine effort later in this chapter (see "Measuring Intensity").

Training in the aerobic threshold zone is perfect for building basic aerobic endurance. This is why aerobic threshold is the dominant intensity during the Base period when developing such fitness is a primary focus. A good portion of each week's training in the Base period should be devoted to zone 2. In the Build period, short-course triathletes should include regular (but less frequent) workouts in zone 2 to maintain aerobic endurance. Long-course athletes will continue to do such workouts frequently in the Build period, since this comes close to simulating the intensity at which they will race.

TRAINING TIME BY INTENSITY ZONE

How much time should you spend in each heart rate zone over the course of a season? This is a question often asked by athletes, and with good reason: Knowing the answer will lead to purposeful and effective training. Unfortunately, it's not an easy question to answer.

The intensity you should aim for in training depends on many different variables. The most important of these is the event for which you are training. There are tremendous differences between preparing for an Ironman-distance triathlon and a sprint-distance race. If we talk in terms of the five basic heart rate zones, it is obvious what our problem is. Preparing for a sprint requires a lot of training near and above the lactate threshold, but for an Ironman-distance race such an effort has no place in training. Ironman training requires a great deal of work around the aerobic threshold. Obviously one cannot train with the same intensities for both events.

Preparing for a sprint requires a lot of training near and above the lactate threshold, but for an Ironman-distance race such an effort has no place in training.

It's not really possible to talk in general about how much time triathletes should spend over the course of the season in each zone, even if we look at each of the four common triathlon distances—sprint, Olympic, half-Ironman, and Ironman. The reason for this is that some people, for example, do a sprint-distance race in less than an hour, while others on the same course and on the same day do it in three hours or more. Regardless of distance, training for a three-hour event is a lot different from training for a one-hour event.

Keep this in mind as you look at Figure 4, which suggests what the distribution of training time by heart rate zone for an entire season might look like. The purpose of this figure is not to give you specific numbers to shoot for, but rather to suggest how your training intensity should be generally distributed. If you can estimate how your intensity might be distributed by zone by the end of the season, you will have an easier time making decisions about how hard to push yourself in workouts.

If we could create a distribution curve for most self-coached athletes, we would probably find that many of them spend a lot more time in the upper heart rate zones for the durations shown in the figures than is advisable. Most athletes push themselves too hard in training. That's the reason injury, overtraining, illness, and burnout are so prevalent in triathlon.

FIGURE 4: Training Volume for Triathlon Races

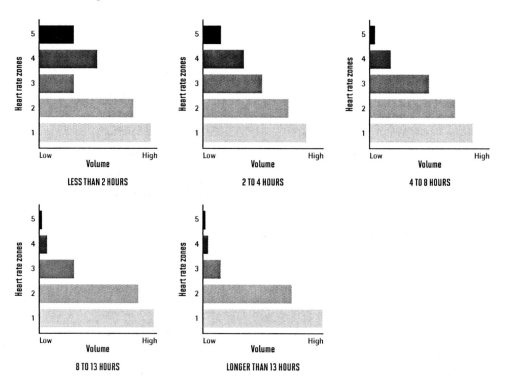

MEASURING INTENSITY

How do you know which intensity zone you are in? Because heart rate monitors are now so common, endurance athletes have come to think of the heart as the best—and perhaps only—indicator of intensity. Such an exaggerated emphasis on heart rate has caused many to forget that it is not the heart rate that limits performance in races and training. As previously explained, fatigue occurs mostly in the muscles, not in the cardiovascular system. The beating of the heart is merely one way to peek into the body to see what is happening. At best, heart rate is an indirect measure of intensity, and not a very sensitive one. There are others that should also be used whenever possible to quantify how intensely you are swimming, biking, or running. Just as with heart rate, each method has shortcomings. By employing two or more methods every time you work out, however, you will learn how to accurately gauge intensity and reap the desired training benefits.

Pace

For the experienced athlete, pace is still, in fact, the best gauge of swimming intensity. For cycling it has less benefit. As for running, it used to be that if you wanted to run at a given pace, there was only one way to do it. You would go to a measured course, such as a track, convert the goal pace into 400-meter or 200-meter splits, and start running. Of course, you wouldn't find out until you completed a split whether you were on pace or not. And then while running you'd have to do the math to figure out just how off-target your pace was and how much to speed up or slow down. Experienced runners developed the ability to gauge exactly how fast they were going based on perceived exertion.

TRIATHLETE'S TRAINING BIBLE
2nd ed.

See pp. 37–38 for Pace-Based Zones for Running and Swimming

Fortunately, technology has made pace training more precise. A wristband GPS device can determine your position, pace, and distance using satellite technology. GPS, short for Global Positioning System, is accurate to within as little as 3 meters, depending on the device you use and how strong of a signal it receives.

Another useful device is the accelerometer. These electromechanical sensors measure movement changes—accelerations—to record pace and distance. For runners they come with a small "pod" that fastens to your shoe.

The accelerometer is built into the pod along with a small transmitter that wirelessly relays the data to a wristwatch where your pace and other information is displayed.

Some devices include other features as well, such as a heart rate monitor, and the capability to download the data to your computer for analysis. Neither a GPS nor an accelerometer is cheap, but prices vary considerably based on the features and functions included.

So which device is right for you? If you run in places where the sky is often blocked out by tall trees or buildings, then an accelerometer is the way to go. The accelerometer is also useful if you run frequently on treadmills. But if you switch shoes for your runs, or don't want to add a tiny amount of weight to your shoe, then the GPS option is better.

TRIATHLETE'S
TRAINING BIBLE
2nd ed.

*See pp. 39–44
for more on
Rating of Perceived
Exertion and Heart
Rate Monitors*

The key with using any such device for training is to think of it only as a tool to help you train more precisely. If you try to "beat" the device, or spend all of your time looking at your wrist rather than paying attention to how you feel, it will detract from, rather than enhance, your running enjoyment and performance.

Two other measures of intensity are perceived exertion and heart rate monitors. Power is another important measure, especially on the bike.

Power

Because there are so many variables on the bike, power is a more objective measure of intensity than pace. Put simply, power is the ability to apply muscular strength. More precisely, it can be defined as

$$\text{Power} = \text{force} \times \text{distance} \div \text{time}$$

On the bike, if you are able to increase the gear size while your cadence remains constant, your power goes up. Your power also increases if you are able to turn the cranks faster with the same gear size. Currently it's not feasible to directly measure power in swimming or running, although the day may come when it is, probably sooner for running. Many multisport athletes, however, are now using power to govern, measure, and analyze cycling intensity. Given that the bike leg is the longest leg of a race, a power meter is a worthwhile investment.

Power is more closely related to performance than any other measure discussed here, and it is therefore an excellent indicator of training workload. The more power you can generate aerobically, the more likely you are to get good results in races. For example, according to one study, the amount of power generated during a 2-minute test is a better indicator of time trial ability on the bike than aerobic capacity (VO$_2$max) is.

I require every triathlete I work with to use a power meter. Why? I know athletes are more likely to achieve their race goals by training—and racing— with power than without. I've seen it happen with every athlete I've coached since power meters hit the market several years ago.

Heart rate monitors are great by themselves, but they're even more beneficial when they can work in conjunction with power. With a power meter, an athlete can compare heart rate with watts (the unit of measure for most power meters, named after James Watt, who invented the steam engine in 1769). Instead of just relying on how he or she feels, the athlete has objective information for establishing intensity.

Power meters remove most of the guesswork that goes into training and racing. For example, many athletes don't consider a work interval to be "started" until their heart rate reaches the targeted level. With a power meter, the interval starts as soon as the power hits the targeted zone—which means right away.

Heart rate monitors teach athletes to focus on the heart, but the muscles are really the key to fitness. This is particularly true when doing intervals. It can be very challenging to get the intensity right in the first minute or so of the first few intervals in a workout. Heart rate can't be relied upon, as it is low and takes the first couple of minutes to rise. But a power meter identifies your intensity level precisely and immediately.

Using a power meter in a long race such as an Ironman is almost like cheating. When everyone else is fighting the wind, flying downwind, or guessing how hard to go when climbing, the triathlete with a power meter is just rolling along at the prescribed power. He or she will produce the fastest possible bike portion of the race—leaving enough energy for the best possible run—because the optimal target power has been determined through training and then followed closely during the race. While something similar can be done with heart rate, there are some confounding factors, such as cardiac drift, the acute effect of diet, and the heart's slow response on hills.

Power meters also provide a highly accurate profile of how fitness changes throughout the season. I test the athletes I coach regularly using a combination of heart rate and power. Without this information I really wouldn't know for sure whether they were making progress. I'd just be guessing.

Unfortunately, power meters aren't cheap. But as with any technology, prices keep falling as the number of options increases. Eventually, just as with heart rate monitors, most multisport athletes will be training with power meters—and racing better because of them. Given the option of buying fast wheels or a power meter, the power meter is the better choice. There is more to be gained from having a powerful engine.

Training with power, just like training with pace, RPE, or a heart rate monitor, requires the use of training zones based on a personal standard. The next chapter will describe how to determine your critical power zones.

TRIATHLETE'S
TRAINING BIBLE
2nd ed.

See pp. 34–44
for more on
Measuring
Intensity

MEASURING FITNESS

This is a good place to begin pulling together some of the intensity concepts in this chapter—aerobic threshold, heart rate, pace, and power. All of them come into play when it comes to determining whether you have done enough aerobic threshold training to consider that aspect of fitness complete.

To make this determination, you will compare heart rate with either power or pace, depending on the sport and your equipment, and see if the two are staying closely linked with little or no cardiac drift. Cardiac drift is the tendency of heart rate to rise even though power or pace remains steady. In an aerobically fit athlete it will be minimal. The following explains an advanced method that you may use to determine if your aerobic fitness is as good as it should be at the end of the Base period. This method is not for everyone. But if you are a serious athlete who enjoys analyzing training data, you can learn a lot about your fitness using this method.

On a bike with a power meter, complete an aerobic threshold ride, then upload the power meter's heart rate and power data to analysis software such as WKO+™, which is available at the Web site TrainingPeaks.com (see additional information later in this chapter, "Using Software to Measure Form, Fitness, and Fatigue"). The software separates the aerobic threshold portion of the ride into two halves in order to compare the first half with the second half. For each half, it will divide average power by average heart rate to establish a ratio. It will then compare the results by subtracting the ratio from the first half of this portion of the ride from the ratio from the second half, and dividing the difference by the ratio from the first half. This produces a percentage of change in the power–to–heart rate from the first half to the second half of the aerobic threshold ride.

Here is an example of how power–to–heart rate ratio percentage of change is calculated:

First half of aerobic threshold portion of ride
Power average: 180 watts
Heart rate average: 135 bpm
First-half power–to–heart rate ratio: *1.33*

Second half of aerobic threshold portion of ride
Power average: 178 watts
Heart rate average: 139 bpm
Second-half power–to–heart rate ratio: *1.28*

Calculating change
Second-half ratio minus first-half ratio: 0.05
The difference is then divided by the first-half ratio: 0.038
Power–to–heart rate shift: *3.8 percent*

If your power–to–heart rate shift is less than 5 percent, as in the above example, the workout is said to be "coupled," meaning the power and heart rate graph lines stay close to parallel, as shown in Figure 5. That's good. But if the shift in the power–to–heart rate ratio is greater than 5 percent, the workout is "decoupled," as shown in Figure 6. Note that the two lines on this graph do not remain parallel for the entire aerobic threshold portion of the workout. That's not good.

FIGURE 5: "Coupled" Aerobic Threshold Workout

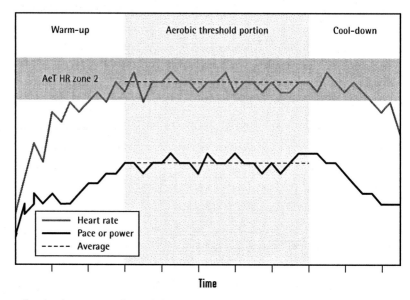

Note how heart rate remains parallel with pace or power.

FIGURE 6: "Decoupled" Aerobic Threshold Workout

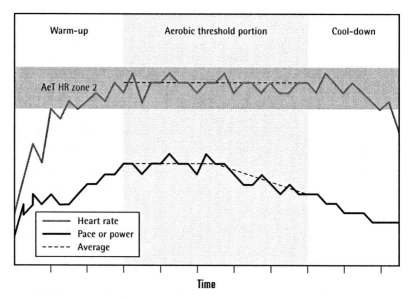

Note how heart rate remains parallel with pace or power for only part of the aerobic threshold portion of the workout. The decline in power indicates a lack of aerobic fitness for long durations.

TABLE 1: Coupling Goals for Aerobic Threshold Portion of Workout

RACE DISTANCE	BIKE (HEART RATE/POWER)	RUN (HEART RATE/PACE)
Sprint	1 hour	30 minutes
Olympic	2 hours	1 hour
Half-Ironman	3 hours	1.5 hours
Ironman	4 hours	2 hours

When aerobic threshold rides or runs at the race-duration goals in Table 1 remain coupled, I consider aerobic threshold fitness fully developed for that length of race and this primary goal of the Base period accomplished. When this happens, an athlete is ready to move on to more advanced training goals. The athlete does need to maintain aerobic threshold endurance even after it is developed, and this can be accomplished by doing such a workout about half as often as was necessary to create it in the first place. Note that being aerobically fit for a sprint-distance race does not mean you are also aerobically fit for longer-distance events, although if you are aerobically fit for a longer race, you are certainly fit enough for shorter ones.

> When aerobic threshold rides or runs at the race-duration goals remain coupled, I consider aerobic threshold fitness fully developed for that length of race and this primary goal of the Base period accomplished.

Gauging Aerobic Threshold

Cycling workout: You can either ride while keeping your heart rate steady to see what happens to your power, or you can maintain a steady power and see what your heart rate does. In the Base period, it's generally better to maintain a steady heart rate, while for the Build period you should keep power steady.

Running workout: Using a GPS device or accelerometer, you can either run while keeping your heart rate steady to see what happens to your pace, or you can maintain a steady pace and see what your heart rate does. In the Base period, it's generally better to maintain a steady heart rate, while for the Build period you should keep pace steady. Aim to stay within that same 5 percent amount of drift. Use Table 3 to determine the duration goal for your aerobic threshold runs.

Determining coupling and decoupling is not possible for swimming as of this writing, as there is no way to accurately measure and analyze pace while swimming. I find that in the pool, heart rate monitors often have dead spots in the data stream due to poor transmission and reception in the water, which results in inaccurate heart rate information. That may well change soon with the rapid growth of digital technology.

Even if you don't have a power meter, GPS, or accelerometer, you can still do the aerobic threshold bike and run workouts using your trusty heart rate monitor. You will have to make decisions about your aerobic endurance fitness based strictly on perceived exertion; over time, the effort at aerobic threshold heart rate will seem to be getting easier.

USING SOFTWARE TO MEASURE FORM, FITNESS, AND FATIGUE

Although the discussion of periodization in Chapter 3 sounds very scientific, training based on periodization is largely a leap of faith. You simply trust that organizing your workouts in a certain way will produce peak readiness on race day. Along the way it is possible to take "snapshots" of your fitness every four weeks or so by doing field tests. But since the physiological changes are generally quite small—on the order of 1 percent—variables such as weather, the warm-up, or even a couple of cups of coffee can easily affect the results. So you are back to trusting your instincts when it comes to assessing whether you are fitter than you were a few weeks ago.

For those who have power meters, that situation is changing for bike training. With new software designed by Hunter Allen and Andrew Coggan, it is possible to graph and manage the daily changes in your race preparation. This is the WKO+ software mentioned earlier, which is available at TrainingPeaks.com, and it is compatible with all power meters.

One of the most powerful features of WKO+ is its performance management chart, which allows you to track periodization and progress toward your race goals. Figure 7 is based on a screen shot of the chart for the early season for one of the athletes I coach. This is a good example of the direction training technology is going. If you are serious about your race performance, you may want to consider downloading this software. When you know exactly how your training is progressing, you can respond quickly when small periodization changes are necessary to stay on track toward your goals.

FIGURE 7: Sample Performance Management Chart from WKO+ Software

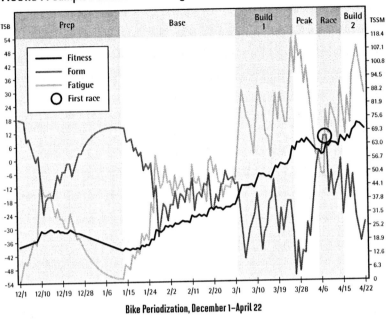

Bike Periodization, December 1–April 22

There are three aspects of training represented by the lines on the graph. These are called "normalized power," "intensity factor," and "training stress score" and reflect the intensity, duration, and frequency of your bike workouts. To learn more about these details, see Allen and Coggan's book *Training and Racing with a Power Meter* (VeloPress 2006).

The light gray line on the chart represents *fatigue*. It closely approximates what you would subjectively describe after a few days of hard training. Notice the spikes and valleys. These indicate alternating hard and easy workout days. The spikes show increased training stress from long, high-intensity, and/or frequent bike workouts. The valleys represent short, easy rides or days off the bike.

The black line is *fitness*. When this line rises, fitness is improving. Notice that it isn't a straight line. Fitness is never static; it is always changing, either positively or negatively. Also, fitness only increases in response to increases in fatigue. Fitness and fatigue go hand in hand. This makes sense, as being fatigued means you trained hard, and hard training produces greater fitness. Although a few days of extended rest are necessary every three or four weeks to prevent overtraining and burnout, you must be careful not to make the break too long, or too much fitness will be lost. The software allows you to monitor these changes. Effectively balancing rest and stress is tricky when it comes to fitness.

The darker gray line represents *form*, which may also be described as race readiness. Form rises when you back off from hard training to rest more. It falls when you train frequently with high-intensity or long workouts. On the left side of the graph, you see a 0 (zero) in the center of the scale. When the "form" line is above this point, the athlete is "on form."

So now let's take a look at the early-season periodization for one of my athletes and see how it worked out. Along the fitness curve I've indicated his early-season periods: Prep, Base, Build, Peak, and Race (indicated with a circle). The second Build period, following the Race period, is the start of his return to hard training in preparation for the next A-priority race on his schedule.

You'll recall that the Prep period is a time when the athlete is just getting back into training following a break at the end of the previous season. In this case, it was December through early January. He had a family vacation planned for the last three weeks of this period and did not have a bike available. Here, since he wasn't riding, you can see the steady drop in both fatigue and fitness. Accompanying that drop is a rise in form. He was really rested—at least as far as the bike goes—but, of course, his bike fitness was rapidly declining.

In the Base period he returned to steady and consistent training. He spent time on the indoor trainer working on aerobic endurance, muscular force, and pedaling speed skills. The steady rise in fatigue and fitness, with a drop in form, indicates that training was going as expected.

During the first Build period, I began to increase the intensity of his training by including muscular endurance rides, made up primarily of intervals and tempo segments, while maintaining his three fitness abilities—endurance, force, and speed skills—established in the Base period. Both fatigue and fitness rose at a greater rate and form dropped to a low point of the early season due to this increase in the training load. I made slight adjustments to stress and rest along the way as the chart revealed how he was responding to training.

In the short Peak period, he did just a couple of hard workouts with lots of rest between them. Notice how fatigue dropped dramatically while fitness decreased only slightly. The most important change to see here is the rapid rise in form, with an increase above the horizontal zero line mentioned above. At his first race, he was not only at a high level of fitness, he was also well rested. This was evident in his sense of being ready on race day and in his race performance. He was *on form.*

Following this first race of the season, he went on a mountain-biking vacation for a few days, and resumed hard training on his return. As you can see on the far right side, he was well on his way to the second peak of the season, which produced even better results.

⎯⎯⎯⎯⎯⎯⎯⎯⎯⎯⎯⎯⎯⎯

Form, fitness, and fatigue cannot be perfectly timed for every race, but they can give you valuable insight into adjustments that need to be made to intensity. Even if you decide not to use a power meter, you can use your training diary and other workout data to track patterns of fatique and recovery.

5: Assessing Fitness

At the end of every triathlon season you should update your personal profile: Begin by ranking your performance within your race category for swimming, biking, and running, using a scale of 1 to 5 (where 1 is worst and 5 is best). Then revisit your Natural Abilities Profile and Mental Skills Profile. These are more subjective measures of your progress as a triathlete, but they are no less important. You can enjoy seeing your competencies develop from year to year and more specifically focus your goals for the next season.

In Chapter 5 of *The Triathlete's Training Bible*, I also presented several objective methods for assessing your personal fitness as well as some tests you should periodically include in your training. These tests provide a baseline at the start of each new season and milestones further down the road.

Yet another essential component making up a comprehensive personal assessment is the medical evaluation.

TRIATHLETE'S TRAINING BIBLE 2nd ed.

See pp. 50–51 for profiles

MEDICAL EVALUATION

I ask all of my athletes to go to a doctor for a complete physical exam at the start of the new season. The older you become, the more important this is. It's most likely that nothing unusual will be found. Then again, your doctor may discover something important, such as skin cancer, high blood pressure, high cholesterol, or prostate or breast cancer. Conditions such as these are much easier to treat in their early stages than they are later on. Getting an annual physical exam is just a good preventative practice, whether someone is an athlete or not, but it is even more important for you as an athlete because you will be putting more stress on your body than the average person. Of course, your doctor will probably give you a clean bill of health.

The more fit you are, the less likely you are to believe there could be something wrong with your health. Ask Lance Armstrong about that. At what he thought was the pinnacle of his career as a cyclist, having won the world road championships, he discovered that he had cancer. Health problems can happen to anyone, no matter how fit they are.

I advise every athlete to also make a preseason appointment with a physical therapist. Look for one who has experience working with endurance athletes. Some insurance plans allow you to go directly to a physical therapist without a doctor's prescription. If your health insurance does not cover such a visit to a physical therapy center, be prepared to pay $100 to $200 for a one-hour screening. What you will learn is well worth the cost.

> Getting an annual physical exam is just a good preventative practice, but it is even more important for you as an athlete because you will be putting more stress on your body than the average person.

The physical therapist will do a head-to-toe exam looking for potential injury sites due to lack of strength, limited flexibility, or physical imbalances. He or she can tell you how to modify your training or how to adjust equipment (such as running shoe orthotics) to allow for your unique weaknesses. Look for a therapist who can also do bike fits, and then can recommend adjustments, including bike-shoe cleat spacers or a bike stem length change.

Everyone has physical imperfections. Common imperfections for triathletes are leg-length discrepancies, weak muscles that allow the body to move from side to side and rotate, tight muscles and tendons, muscle imbalances, limited range of motion in the joints, poor posture, and scoliosis. These may be hereditary, caused by a fall or other trauma to the body, or simply a result of the repetitive motions of swimming, biking, and running. The physical therapist can also suggest strengthening or stretching exercises to correct these imperfections.

At this time, you may wish to make an appointment with a lab for metabolic testing as well (see details below). This type of testing can provide you with information that will be valuable in designing your training program.

Once you have the general health exam, the physical therapy exam, and the metabolic testing behind you, it will be time to evaluate yourself specifically for high-level cycling performance.

LAB TESTING

At least once each year, generally in the early Base period, I send my athletes to the lab for metabolic testing, sometimes called gas analysis. Athletes usually refer to this as a "VO_2max test," but it goes well beyond discovering your VO_2max. Most think this test reveals their potential for high-level performance. It does not tell you this any more than competing in a race shows your potential for future races. But this test does quantify your current level of fitness from many different angles.

Metabolic testing assesses your current fitness level and can also provide useful information about heart rate zones, bike power zones, run pace zones, how much fat and carbohydrate you use at various intensities, and how efficient your sport-specific skills are when swimming, pedaling a bike, or running, depending on the tested sport. Lab testing also helps establish your personal rating of perceived exertion (RPE) on a given scale (for example, a scale of 1 to 10, where 1 is easy and 10 is hard) so that you can think about effort more precisely in the future. All of this will help fine-tune your training plan.

That's a lot to be gained from one test session that takes only about an hour to complete. If you are self-coached, the technician can help you make sense of the test results and may even offer suggestions on how to use the information to train more effectively.

All of this generally costs in the range of $100 to $200. Look for a facility that specializes in athlete testing, not one that caters to those at risk for heart disease or aging populations. These tests are becoming more readily available in health clubs, physical therapy centers, and bike, running, and triathlon stores. Some coaches even provide such a service.

By repeating the test at the start of each major period of the season, especially the Base 1, Build 1, and Peak periods, you can closely monitor your training progress. These tests also serve as great motivators when you don't have a race scheduled for some time.

CRITICAL POWER TESTS

One of the tests included in Chapter 5 showed you how to use a power meter to establish power-based training zones. To review, you can define your critical power profile with just four time trials of 1, 6, 12, and 30 minutes. Each test is a maximum effort for the entire duration. Each test should be conducted when you are rested, so you should spread them out over several days.

To estimate 60-minute power, subtract 5 percent from your 30-minute average power result. For an approximation of 90-minute power, subtract 2.5 percent from the 60-minute power. Subtracting 5 percent from the 90-minute power figure estimates 180-minute power.

TRIATHLETE'S
TRAINING BIBLE
2nd ed.

*See p. 64
for more on
Critical Power Tests*

TABLE 2: Critical Power Zone Benefits and Race Applications

DURATION	CP ZONES	FITNESS BENEFIT	RACE APPLICATION
12 sec.	CP0.2	Explosive power	Finishing sprint
			Short hill
			Start
1 min.	CP1	Lactate clearance	Fast starts
			Short climbs
6 min.	CP6	Velocity at VO$_2$max	Moderate-duration climbs
			Short, high-intensity segments
12 min.	CP12	Aerobic capacity (VO$_2$max)	Deeply anaerobic
30 min.	CP30	Lactate superthreshold	Long, steady efforts
60 min.	CP60	Lactate threshold	Short-duration race endurance
90 min.	CP90	Sublactate threshold	Moderate-duration race
180 min.	CP180	Basic aerobic function	Long-duration race endurance

Once your 60-minute CP is established, you can use it as the basis for determining your power training zones as shown in Table 3.

TABLE 3: Power Zones Based on Percentages of CP60

ZONE 1	ZONE 2	ZONE 3	ZONE 4	ZONE 5	ZONE 6	ZONE 7
Recovery	Aerobic	Tempo	Threshold	Aerobic Capacity	Anaerobic Capacity	Power
<56%	56–75%	76–90%	91–105%	106–120%	121–150%	>150%

As your triathlon career progresses, it is important to go back and reassess to see how your abilities have evolved. The tests included in this chapter will assist you in making an objective as opposed to a subjective evaluation of your progress as a multisport athlete. In addition to the Natural Abilities Profile and Mental Skills Profile mentioned earlier, this chapter contains several time trial and graded exercise tests for swimming, cycling, and running.

TRIATHLETE'S
TRAINING BIBLE
2nd ed.

See pp. 53–59 for
Fitness Tests

6: Building Fitness

This chapter talks about a variety of ways to improve fitness, including ways to train both basic and advanced abilities and to focus on your limiters. Limiters are race-specific weaknesses that must be resolved in order to improve your performance in competitive events.

RACE RESULTS AND LIMITERS

You probably already have a good sense of what your weakest sport is. If you are unsure, race results can help you decide. Look at your rankings from recent races. Do you see a pattern? For example, if finishing 18th in the swim, 14th in the bike leg, and 6th in the run is a typical ranking for you, then swimming is a primary limiter, with cycling being second. You will probably want to improve your swimming.

TRIATHLETE'S
TRAINING BIBLE
2nd ed.

See pp. 74–78 for more on Limiters and Racing

But hold on: The decision may not be quite so simple. You also need to consider how much time you could gain by becoming a more proficient swimmer. Again, use your race results to determine this. If you could become a good enough swimmer to move up from 18th place in the swim to perhaps 10th, how much time would you gain? Examine the results to see what the time of the 10th-place athlete's swim was. Let's say you might gain a minute by devoting more training resources to swimming. A minute is a lot, so that would be good. But if you look at the bike times in the same way, you may find that by moving from 14th to 10th place you could save 2 minutes.

So while swimming may be your weakest sport, cycling is where you stand to shave the most time; from a risk/reward perspective, cycling is the sport to invest in. This doesn't mean you should ignore your weakness in swimming. You should still work to develop any limiters you have. It's just that by putting more of your resources into cycling you may reap a greater reward in future races.

Most limiters require you to focus your training more on speed skills.

Most limiters require you to focus your training more on speed skills. It could be that you are seeing your race results hit a plateau and no matter how smart or targeted your training becomes, you cannot break through that wall. In times like these, speed skills can prove essential to your improvement as a triathlete. What if better technique allowed you to become more efficient? That efficiency could lead to faster racing.

It's really quite simple. To run faster all you have to do is increase your leg turnover or lengthen your stride. In fact, running speed may be expressed as a formula using only these two variables:

$$\text{Run speed} = \text{stride rate} \times \text{stride length}$$

The same may be said for riding a bike fast, but now we use gear size instead of stride length:

$$\text{Bike speed} = \text{stroke rate} \times \text{gear size}$$

So to ride a bike fast, you can either turn the pedals around at a high rate, use a high gear, or do a little of both.

And it's no different for swimming:

$$\text{Swim speed} = \text{stroke rate} \times \text{stroke length}$$

That's all there is to it.

Well, actually, in the real world of triathlon there's more to it than just that. There is this other stuff that exercise physiologists talk about that makes up fitness called aerobic capacity (VO_2max), lactate threshold, and economy of movement. These markers of fitness make it possible to keep the cadence high, the stride or stroke long, and the gear high for a long time. Of these the most highly trainable for the fit athlete is economy of movement—or pedaling, in the world of cycling.

Economy of movement essentially refers to how much effort you're using when swimming, biking, or running at a given pace. By improving your economy you can go faster at the same effort. In Chapter 12 of this *Companion* we'll explore this ability in much greater detail.

Economy of movement is largely determined by biomechanics—how efficiently you move the various body parts while swimming, biking, and running. This is a nervous system function. It does not have anything to do with how great your aerobic capacity and lactate threshold are. Since economy has nothing to do with these aerobic and anaerobic functions, training requires a different way of thinking. Breathing hard does not improve the functioning of the nervous system. Nor does fatigue. When it comes to improving speed skills, you must avoid both of these common side effects of endurance training, as they will prevent you from improving your biomechanics.

Improving biomechanics requires concentrating on making a few precise movement patterns and then taking a relatively long rest break before trying it again. After repeating this pattern several times, it's best to call it a day before fatigue sets in and you get sloppy. If you've ever tried to learn a skill-oriented sport—such as golf, tennis, or fly-fishing—you know what I mean. Once technique begins to break down, you are no longer refining the skill—you're simply ingraining bad habits.

For example, good pedaling skills are based on a slight amount of "ankling" (see Figure 8). This means using your ankle like a movable hinge instead of a rigid crowbar. On flat terrain, during the upstroke the ankle slowly opens, allowing the heel to rise slightly above the toes (position H). On the downstroke the ankle closes a bit so that the heel is even with or slightly below the toes (position B). On a climb, ankling may be slightly more pronounced. Figure 8 illustrates pedaling mechanics.

FIGURE 8: Pedaling Biomechanics, Position and Force

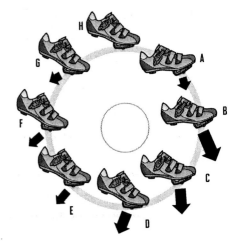

The downside of changing your biomechanics is that initially you will get slower or feel like you are working harder. This may last several weeks but will gradually turn around. When it does you will go faster at the same effort. Hang in there until then.

7: Planning a Year

Y ou may recall from *The Triathlete's Training Bible* that there are several steps to follow in creating an Annual Training Plan. They are:

1. Determine your goals for the upcoming season.
2. Establish objectives that will support your goals.
3. Establish your annual training hours.
4. Prioritize your planned races.
5. Divide your season into training periods.
6. Assign hours to each week of training.

Planning your season and actually following the plan are two entirely separate things. There are a number of pitfalls awaiting you once you have a plan in hand and start to train. Let's examine them.

CHANGING THE ANNUAL TRAINING PLAN

Once you have created an Annual Training Plan, there are two common blunders you must avoid. The first is the more common—ignoring the plan and simply training as you always have. I hope that once you've put in the time to create a solid plan, one that will help produce your best race results ever, you won't disregard it. That would be a considerable waste of both your planning time and your training time. The second mistake is the opposite— to pay *too much* attention to the plan and not make changes when dictated by new circumstances. I'm not talking about circumstances like wanting to go on the group ride on a scheduled rest day. I mean those times when you realize that you are making inadequate progress, or you begin missing workouts because something unexpected has happened. Be realistic in these situations and adapt the plan as needed.

Inadequate Progress

When you're not making the progress you had expected, you must make strategic changes in your plan. You'll know whether you're making progress because you will perform a test and compare the results

A common cause of poor progress is simply doing the wrong sort of training.

with your training objectives as described in Step 2 above. The test could be a field test, a test done in a clinic, or a C-priority race. Figure 9 shows how to handle the results. Basically, you will compare them with your planned objectives and see if you are on track or not quite up to par. If your progress is good, you will continue following the plan. If you're not happy with your progress, reevaluate the plan and decide what must change.

What could need changing? It could be that you didn't spend enough time in the Base period and some of your basic abilities are lacking. This is the most common mistake athletes make—they can't wait to get to the hard training of the Build period, so they cut the Base period short. The solution is simply to go back to Base 3 for a few weeks to strengthen endurance, force, and speed skills. Of these, if you have made the Base period shorter than it should have been, poor endurance is the most likely problem.

FIGURE 9: Planning and Implementation Model

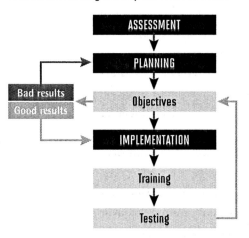

Or it may be that your objectives, and perhaps even your goals, were set unrealistically high. This mistake is especially common among athletes who are in their first few years of triathlon. After you've had a chance to implement the plan and test your progress, it may become clear that you expected too much. Give some thought to revising your goals and objectives at this point.

Another common cause of poor progress is simply doing the wrong sort of training. The problem may be that you are spending too much time training your strengths while giving your limiters only lip service. As explained in Chapter 6 of the Training Bible, the focus of most of your training must be on those race-specific weaknesses—limiters—that are holding you back. The tendency among self-coached athletes is to spend more training time on what they are already good at than on their weaknesses. Realize that it is only by training in your limiters that you will obtain better results.

Another common problem is the inclusion of too many group workouts in your training. If you are going along with the group, you may not be focusing on what you really need to get out of that workout session. There are times when having training partners can be very beneficial, but group workouts are often detrimental, especially in the Base period. You may be working either too hard or too easy, depending on the skills and experience of your training partners. Look for partners who are of similar ability, and decide on a workout before starting. Unstructured group workouts tend to become "races." In the Build period this may be beneficial, but only if done in moderation. If your workout objectives are compatible with those of the group, then go ahead and take advantage of the camaraderie.

Missing Workouts—or More

It happens to everyone. Your training is going well, you've been consistent, and you can tell that your fitness is progressing. Then your job throws you a curve ball and you have to miss a day or more of training. Or you catch a winter virus and don't train for four days while your body is fighting it off. Maybe your knee becomes inflamed and the doctor says no running or cycling for two weeks, or you decide you're too tired to train and need an extra day off. What should you do? Should you try to fit in the missed workouts at a later time by wedging them in between the others? Or do you just continue on as if nothing happened? How will this affect your race preparation? Here is how to handle such dilemmas.

Missing three or fewer days. For downtime of just a few days, continue training with no adjustments. The worst thing you can do is to try to fit in the lost workouts. That will not only set you up for poor training quality due to accumulated fatigue but also increase the potential for a breakdown, such as an overuse injury, an illness, or the early stages of overtraining.

Missing four to seven days. If you've missed more than a few days, some rearranging is required. You'll need to readjust your workouts for up to two weeks, but you won't be able to do all of the missed workouts plus those originally planned over that time period. You'll need to be selective. The most important workouts to retain are the ones related to your limiters. Reorganize your schedule so that you can do most of those, although that may mean skipping some of the workouts that maintain your strengths. Be sure to include easy days just as you would normally do in training. Don't try to cram more hard training into fewer days.

Missing one to two weeks. If you miss one or two weeks of training, step back one mesocycle and omit an entire chunk of the training you had planned to do in the future, rather than trying to merge the lost workouts into your existing plan. For example, say you missed two weeks of training in Build 2. When ready to train normally again, go back to Build 1 for two weeks and do the appropriate workouts. Adjust your plan by cutting out two weeks of training that were scheduled to take place later in the season. One way to do this is to make Build 2 three weeks long instead of four and to omit Peak 1.

Missing more than two weeks. Missing a significant block of time, such as two weeks or more, requires a return to the Base period, as one or more of the basic abilities—endurance, force, or speed skills—have probably been compromised. If you were already in the Base period when the training time was lost, step back one mesocycle. Let's say you were in Base 3 and had to miss three weeks of training for some reason. Return to Base 2. If you were in Build 2 when it happened, go back to Base 3 and then continue on from this new starting point. You will need to make major revisions to your Annual Training Plan to accommodate this change by omitting some portion of Build 2 and by possibly shortening the Peak period from two weeks to one.

No matter which of these unfortunate situations occurs, you will have less fitness on race day than you had originally hoped. You can't force in the extra workouts, because there is a limit to how much stress your body can handle. You can't force it to become just as fit on less training. This is why it is so important to avoid taking high risks in training; if you become injured, you could miss critical training hours while forced to take time off to recuperate. In any case, remember that missing some training isn't a disaster; it's simply a situation that you need to manage. Adjust your plan and move on.

Never Compromise Recovery

By now you know that consistency is the key to success in athletic training. If you train inconsistently as a result of frequent physical breakdowns or mental burnout, you will never achieve a high level of race readiness. To maintain consistent training, you must provide adequate recovery days every week. One of those days should be very light. For a triathlete who trains fewer than 10 hours each week, this could mean a day off; for someone who does 15 hours a week, it could mean doing an hour of weight lifting instead of riding; and for a 25-hour-per-week triathlete, it could mean a two-hour, easy ride. The other weekly recovery workouts should be done at a low intensity—for example, in heart rate zone 2.

There are two common ways to blend recovery days and high-stress training days within a week. For the triathlete who is fairly new to the sport or who recovers slowly, as most older athletes do, alternating hard and easy days generally works best. For example, such an athlete may follow a weekly pattern like this:

Monday	Day off
Tuesday	Two or three long or intense workouts
Wednesday	One or two short, low-intensity workouts
Thursday	Two or three long or intense workouts
Friday	One or two short, low-intensity workouts
Saturday	One or two long and/or high-intensity workouts
Sunday	One or two very long, moderate-intensity workouts

On the other hand, an experienced triathlete or one who recovers very quickly might benefit from grouping high-stress workouts on back-to-back days and then taking a break by having an easy day for recovery:

Monday	Day off or light training
Tuesday	Two or three long or intense workouts
Wednesday	Two or three long or intense workouts
Thursday	Two or three long or intense workouts
Friday	One or two short, low-intensity workouts
Saturday	One or two long and/or high-intensity workouts
Sunday	One or two very long, moderate-intensity workouts

Not everyone respects recovery days. I often see self-coached athletes miss workouts or become frustrated with their progress, then overcompensate by making their recovery days harder. That's exactly the wrong thing to do. You will only create more fatigue and lower your workout quality on the harder days. The solution in this case is to make the hard training days harder and the easy days easier. Making workouts harder means either making them longer, doing them at a higher intensity, or doing more high-intensity volume, such as more intervals. Whatever your approach, never compromise recovery to gain fitness. It doesn't work.

8: Planning a Week

The subject of this chapter is understanding and applying the principles of workout scheduling. It will help you determine the key workouts for each week of the season and have a good understanding of how they blend into a weekly schedule.

TIMING YOUR WORKOUTS

Any suggested system of scheduling specific days on which to swim, bike, run, or do combined workouts or weight workouts may not work for your particular lifestyle, job, facility availability, and training groups. How then do you schedule your training sessions? By taking all of the above factors into account and designing your own customized training week, one that you can repeat week after week for the entire season with only minor changes as new circumstances arise. Here's how to do that.

> To schedule your training sessions, take all of the factors into account and design your own customized training week that you can repeat week after week for the entire season with only minor changes as new circumstances arise.

Anchor Workouts

These are workouts that must occur on given days each week and over which you have little or no control. For example, if your masters group swims on Tuesdays, Thursdays, and Saturdays, those are the sessions you must plug into your weekly plan. Likewise, if you swim alone but the pool is only available for lap swimming on Mondays, Wednesdays, and Fridays, that is when these anchor workouts must be placed in your weekly plan. Other typical anchor workouts are group bike or run sessions that are scheduled for certain times and days each week. Your longest bike ride and longest run may also be anchor workouts because you typically must do these on the weekend when you have more time available.

Time-Flexible Workouts

Next, you'll schedule in the remaining workouts, those that are not anchors and may be done on any day of the week. If you are a high-training-volume athlete and do four or more workouts per sport each week, then putting them on your calendar will be fairly easy—just list two workouts a day and be done with it. But if you do only two or three weekly sessions in a given sport, then how you space them is important. For example, if you run only two times a week, you would not want those sessions to be on Tuesday and Wednesday, as that leaves five consecutive days without running. With that many days off, you would lose any physical gains that you made during the two workouts. In this case, you should separate the two runs with two to three days of no running. This could mean running, for example, on Tuesdays and Fridays.

With three workouts in a given sport, separate each with a day off from that sport. For example, run on Tuesdays, Thursdays, and Saturdays.

Daily Order of Workouts

Now you'll fine-tune the order of your daily workouts. This is where your appetite for risk and reward will play out. With the anchor workouts, the time of day will probably already be established. But with the flexible workouts there is a primary concern that must be addressed: when you run. It bears repeating that running is the sport in which you are most likely to get injured, due to the extraordinary stress it places on bones, muscles, tendons, and cartilage. If you get a running injury and have to miss several days or even weeks of training, then much, if not all, of your fitness gains will be lost. You need to treat run workouts with caution and do everything you can to prevent injury. One of the most common causes of running injuries is running on tired legs, especially during long or fast runs. You must ensure that your legs are relatively fresh going into these workouts.

Leg fatigue can be a problem anytime you are doing a long or fast run within 24 hours of another challenging run or a bike ride. For example, it is best not to do a long bike ride on Saturday and then follow that with a long run on Sunday. Many triathletes attempt this, believing they are preparing themselves for what will happen in a race when they must run on tired legs. The fatigue experienced the day after a big ride, however, is not the same feeling you will have on race day. In reality, there are many causes of fatigue, as explained in Chapter 4. Your risk of injury is magnified several times over when you take a long run the day after a long bike ride. The solution is to schedule your long run the day before your long ride. So if these are anchor workouts for the weekend, do your long run on Saturday and your long ride on Sunday.

In the same way, you must be cautious with combination workouts, which are known as "bricks." Although combining a long bike ride with a long run may be similar to what you must do in a race, it is also very risky. If you are prone to getting running-related injuries, this is not a good combination for you, and I'd suggest alternating two other types of brick workouts—bike emphasis and run emphasis. In a bike-emphasis brick, you will do a long ride followed by a short run, such as a 15-minute one. Although that is very short, it accomplishes one of the goals of a brick workout—learning to run effectively and efficiently when you have just gotten off the bike. This combination works well for Ironman-distance triathletes. The run-emphasis brick starts with a short bike ride, which may include a few race-intensity efforts. "Short" means 30 to 90 minutes, depending on your weekly volume. The run may then be a long one.

Time Between Workouts

Finally, it's time to schedule some downtime. If you are doing two or more separate workouts—not bricks—in the same day, it is generally best to provide for some rest between them. There may well be some lifestyle circumstances that prevent this, such as when you must fit in a run and swim before going to work in the morning. But generally you will reap greater benefits from your training if you are at least partially recovered from the previous session before starting the next, even though they are in different sports. The time between workouts should include refueling and is best spent sitting down whenever possible.

Given all of the above, you should now be able to design a customized training week that makes the best use of your available time and produces the greatest possible race readiness given your lifestyle.

ONE WORKOUT OR TWO?

Are two workouts as good as one? Is it just as good for you, for example, to do two 45-minute runs as it is to do one 90-minute run? The answer depends on the purpose of the workout. If your objective is to improve your endurance for long events, the answer is no. But if you want to improve any other ability, such as speed skills, force, muscular endurance, or anaerobic endurance, the answer is yes. In fact, for these purposes two runs on the same day are far better than a single long run.

Most triathletes want to improve their endurance, though, so for multisport training, two workouts on the same day are seldom beneficial. Here's why. The physiological benefits of endurance workouts require that you stress not only the many parts of the aerobic system—primarily the heart, lungs, and blood—but also the muscular and nervous systems. In addition, energy, hormone, and enzyme production improvements are necessary for aerobic fitness. Longer workouts are better for stimulating the development of all of the body's aerobic endurance functions. There is also a psychological benefit that comes from completing long workouts.

When it comes to endurance, one long workout beats two short ones.

One reason that one long workout is better than two short ones for improving aerobic endurance has to do with how the body produces energy from fat and carbohydrate during moderate-intensity exercise. As you start a workout, the body relies heavily on carbohydrate stores to provide energy for exercise. But as the duration of the workout increases, there is a steady shift from burning carbohydrate to burning fat. This fat-burning condition is one of the benefits we hope to get from aerobic exercise in order to improve endurance. So if you do two 45-minute runs in the same day rather than one 90-minute run, you will spend less time that day using fat for fuel, and therefore the workouts will produce less of a benefit for the energy-production system. The same example may be applied to the other systems listed above. So when it comes to endurance, one long workout beats two short ones.

RISK ANALYSIS

As we discussed in Chapter 5, each workout you do has associated risks and rewards. Before you begin fleshing out your daily workouts schedule, it's a good idea to step back and reevaluate the degree of risk you are willing to take on and capable of sustaining. Some workouts are low-risk but also produce a low return on your investment of time and energy. Other workouts are risky but can produce dramatic results if you are wise and "invest" in them cautiously. The risks associated with breakthrough workouts are overtraining, injury, illness, and burnout. When these setbacks occur, overly aggressive athletes must return to basic, low-risk, low-reward training in order to reestablish their foundation of fitness. Athletes who experience these conditions frequently are probably addicted to high-risk training and should reexamine their priorities and methods. Figure 10 illustrates the workout risk and reward curves.

FIGURE 10: Risk and Reward in Training

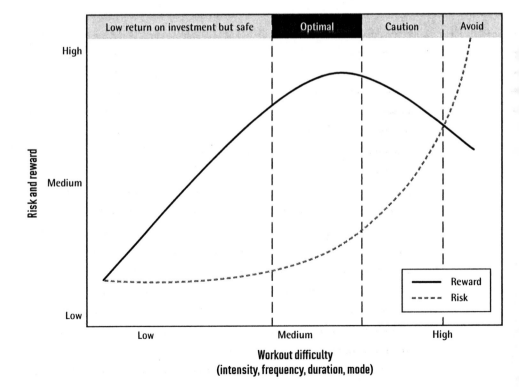

Risk as associated with training comes from some combination of the frequency, intensity, duration, and mode of training and is unique for each athlete. What is high-risk for one athlete may be low-risk for another. The difference has to do with experience, fitness levels, susceptibility to injury, previous training adaptations, age, and other factors.

Each athlete has a workout frequency that is optimal. An elite triathlete may work out three times a day for several days in a row and become more fit. But a novice triathlete trying to do three-a-days will soon break down. An athlete who gets "too much too soon" is forced to stop training for several days in order to recover. It's imperative that you find a workout frequency that works for you and then stick to it.

The same holds true for the intensity and duration of workouts. A lot of training done at high intensity, such as intervals on consecutive days in the same sport, is very risky but potentially rewarding. Extremely long workouts, such as four-hour runs or seven-hour bike rides, are also very risky but potentially rewarding. Taking these risks before you are ready for them can be a big mistake; in fact, doing workouts that are excessive, particularly in terms of duration, is the most common training mistake that self-coached, long-course athletes make.

Risk associated with "mode" refers to the type of workout you do— swim, bike, run, or crosstraining. Of the three triathlon sports, running is the riskiest because of the stress it places on bone and soft tissues. For some athletes, a lot of running can lead to injury, but with the right precautions, the risk can be reduced. This means strengthening running-related tissues and bone gradually. For most athletes, swimming is the least risky of the three triathlon sports.

The risk of injury due to high frequency, intensity, or duration is also minimized when an athlete includes sufficient recovery time in his or her training program. Whenever you work out in the same sport for two consecutive training sessions, be sure to include recovery time. Frequent recovery is the key to keeping this type of risk at a manageable level.

Strength training also can be a high-risk mode of training. Going to high-load weight lifting before the body is ready can easily cause injury, especially if an athlete becomes too aggressive with the risks he or she takes in the weight room.

Within a weight training regimen, some exercises are riskier than others. Freebar squats, for example, can be troublesome. A heavily loaded bar placed on the shoulders can be especially risky for the athlete who is new to the weight room, has experienced knee or hip injuries, or is older and has degenerating spinal disks. But if you can handle it, the reward reaped from squats is significant. Less risky but also less rewarding are exercises that work similar muscle groups as in squats, such as leg presses, step-ups, and lunges.

Plyometric exercises—explosive movements done to build power, especially for running—are also both high-risk and high-reward. Eccentric-contraction plyometrics are riskier but potentially more rewarding than concentric-contraction plyometrics. An example of an eccentric-contraction plyometric exercise is jumping off a high box, landing on the floor, and then immediately springing back up to a second high box. A concentric-contraction version of this same exercise eliminates the jump down and landing. There is less potential for reward this way, but also less risk of injury. For more on how to incorporate plyometrics in your training, refer to the "Complex Training" section in *Companion* Chapter 13.

When selecting a workout, you need to consider the reward that you hope to derive from it as well as the risk involved in performing it. By investing wisely in your training, you can increase your likelihood of building excellent fitness while avoiding the common pitfalls of overly aggressive triathlon training. If you make a mistake in your training, make it on the side of low risk rather than high risk. I guarantee that if you do, you will do better in the long term.

9: Planning to Race

One way of developing comprehensive self-coaching skills is to study how others have put together their annual and weekly plans. The case studies we considered in *The Triathlete's Training Bible* are based on real-world athletes with high aspirations, limited time, and great commitment. I hope their stories have helped you see other options for setting up your season. Of course those plans are not the only possibilities, but they are sound and potentially effective. Regardless of your goal race distance, I suggest that you read all of the case studies because they may offer you new insights into the process of planning.

One of these case studies in Chapter 9 of the *Training Bible* mapped out a full year of training for an athlete preparing for an Ironman-distance triathlon. If you are training for an Ironman, you will undoubtedly be looking for indications that your training is on track.

I've included a list of benchmark workouts that my athletes have found to be helpful. Whether your goal is to simply finish the race or to have a fast race time, these workouts will be a good test of your endurance and a valuable opportunity to refine your pacing and refueling strategies. Once you master these, you can use the "Big Day" training to simulate the stresses of race day.

TRIATHLETE'S
TRAINING BIBLE
2nd ed.

*See pp. 122–125
for Ironman-
Distance Triathlon
case study*

IRONMAN BENCHMARK WORKOUTS

Once you've refined your pacing and refueling strategies, you will be ready to write a race plan. Be sure to stick to it on race day.

Race Goal: Finish an Ironman

Swimming Benchmark Workout: Plan two open-water swims in the last eight weeks before your race—swim with a partner, a following boat, or a lifeguard onshore. You should be able to swim nonstop for 40 minutes with seven weeks to go and for 60 minutes with three weeks remaining.

Not on Target? If you can't complete these benchmark swims, find a swim instructor to help you with your technique. You are undoubtedly wasting too much energy.

Cycling Benchmark Workout: Starting eleven weeks before the race, do a long ride two out of every three weeks. This means you will get in six such rides before the race. Starting eleven weeks out, you should be able to ride three and a half hours. Add about 30 minutes each time. Do your last long ride three weeks before the race; it should be about six hours. Eat and drink exactly as you will in the race.

Not on Target? If you find it difficult to finish any of these long rides, you are either trying to ride too fast early in the workout, not taking in enough calories, or both. Make adjustments in pacing and refueling until you get it just right. Then follow that pattern *exactly* in the race. Do *not* inflate your goal the week of the race.

Running Benchmark Workout: Your goal is to finish the run—not to see how fast you can go. Combine walking and running just as you will do in the race. Complete a long run two out of every three weeks, so that you get in six of these endurance workouts before the race, just as you did with cycling. It's best to space these long bike and long run workouts so that you have at least 48 hours between them each week. If that's not possible, then do the long run the day before the long ride—not the other way around. The first such run should be at least an hour and a half. Add 15 to 20 minutes each time you run until you build to a three-hour workout with three to four weeks to go before the race. Do not go longer than three hours.

Not on Target? If you find it almost unbearable to finish your long run every time you attempt it, then you are either trying to run too fast, you are not walking enough, or you are not taking in enough calories. Gradually refine your run pacing and refueling strategy after each long workout until you have it nailed down tightly. Then be sure to stick to your plan on race day.

Race Goal: Fast Ironman

Swimming Benchmark Workout: Warm up for 10 minutes in a pool. Then swim 500 meters six times with 30-second recoveries. The pace on each 500 should be your race goal pace. If you expect to go out fast in the first 500 meters of the race to get into position, then swim the first 500 of this set at that effort, and settle into the slower pace on the subsequent sets. Record your split times for each 500. Do this workout twice in your Build period, once on each of the "Big Days" (see section, "Ironman Big Day").

Not on Target? Is your 500-meter time remaining constant within a few seconds for the last five intervals? It should be. If not, then you are going too fast early in the set and need to pace yourself. Consider whether your goal pace is realistic.

Cycling Benchmark Workout: After a few weeks of building your longest weekly ride to five or six hours, you will be ready for long aerobic threshold rides. Do four to six of these, with two of them on your "Big Days." These long race simulations will prepare you physically and mentally for the stresses of the race. Warm up for 30 minutes and then ride steadily for two to four hours. Gradually increase the duration over several weeks. Stay in the upper half of heart rate zone 2 for the entire two- to four-hour period of each ride. Or, with a power meter, ride at 65 to 75 percent of your functional threshold power. Cool down for 30 minutes. Be sure to eat and drink exactly as you will do in the race.

Not on Target? These aerobic threshold rides are essentially race-effort simulations done at goal race intensity. If you can't maintain a steady effort for two to four hours, you won't be able to do it in the race for a longer time. So reduce the target heart rate or power until you have it dialed in by the time you ride for four hours. The last such ride should occur three to four weeks before race day.

Running Benchmark Workout: Two out of every three weeks, starting eleven weeks before the race, complete a long run of two and a half to three hours, so that you do six such long runs before the race. In each of them a portion is run at aerobic threshold in the upper half of heart rate zone 2. Three to four weeks before the race, this aerobic threshold portion should be two hours long within the longer run time. Build up to that two-hour portion over the course of the four to six long runs. It's best to separate the long rides and runs by at least 48 hours each week. If that doesn't work with your lifestyle, then do the long run the day before the long ride. This will reduce your risk of injury.

Not on Target? If you are wearing a GPS watch or accelerometer, notice whether your pace is remaining steady. If you are slowing down appreciably even when your heart rate remains constant, then start more conservatively on your next such run. It is also possible that you are not taking in enough calories. By the last long run you should have a good idea of what your Ironman goal pace and heart rate should be.

IRONMAN BIG DAY

Training for an Ironman must include a challenging training event that occurs twice during the season: the "Big Days." As the name implies, a Big Day is intended to significantly simulate the stresses of race day. It tests your preparation in every way. One of your Big Days should occur about eight weeks prior to your Ironman-distance race and the other one about four weeks before the race. It's best to space these stressful days out like this so that you can have several days of recovery after each one. *This workout should only be done by triathletes who are competitive within their categories. Ironman "finishers" can do the workout but at a lower intensity than described below.*

TRIATHLETE'S
TRAINING BIBLE
2nd ed.

*See pp. 255–259
for Pre-Race
Breakfast*

Start the day just as you plan to do on race day by eating your pre-race breakfast. See Chapter 16 of the *Training Bible* for more details on this. Then, at about race start time, swim for 60 to 75 minutes (in open water, if possible). This swim should include long race-effort sets with short recoveries. My favorite for this day is six 500-meter swims with 30-second recoveries done at goal race pace.

After your swim, rest for 90 minutes and eat a light meal. Follow this with a bike ride of five hours, preferably on a course that simulates the terrain you'll encounter on Iron-race day. Warm up for about 30 minutes, then ride for four hours steady in heart rate zone 2 or at 65 to 75 percent of your functional threshold power. Set up your bike just as it will be on race day, ride in an aerodynamic position, and use the same clothing, shoes, and equipment you will use on race day. Eat, drink, and supplement with sodium *exactly* as you will do in the race.

After the ride, rest for 90 minutes and eat a light, mostly liquid meal. Then start a two-hour run on a course as similar to the racecourse as possible. Warm up for 15 to 30 minutes and then start a 90-minute run in heart rate zone 2 or at goal race pace. Eat, drink, and supplement with sodium *exactly* as you intend to do in the race.

This is roughly an eight-hour training day that gives you a taste of what it will be like on race day. But knowing how driven Ironman triathletes are, I probably should emphasize that you should *not* attempt to do the full eight hours nonstop. Be sure to take the two 90-minute breaks, and be sure to refuel and rehydrate during this time. Doing this workout continuously is just too stressful and would require far too long of a recovery.

When you do your two Big Days eight weeks and four weeks before your Ironman event, you'll likely discover some things that need adjusting, such as pacing, equipment, and nutrition. Make the changes and you're that much closer to having a rewarding Ironman.

For more on Big Days and Ironman training refer to *Going Long: Training for Ironman-Distance Triathlons,* 2nd edition (VeloPress, 2009), a book I coauthored with Gordon Byrn, who has taught me a lot about Ironman-distance training and racing.

10: Racing

The most common error for serious multisport athletes is continuing to train at a high workload just before a race in the mistaken belief that race form is improved only by hard work. It isn't so. Form improves during rest. Rest does have its shortcomings, though, so as odd as it may sound, you need to know how to rest the right way. It's best to find a balance point between your normal training workload and rest during race week. This chapter examines that issue and takes you through final race-day preparation, the race itself, and post-race activities. Let's start with your race plan.

THE RACE PLAN

Having the performance and race results you want in an A-priority race largely depends on having an effective strategy. A race strategy is nothing more than a plan that covers the race-day variables over which you have control. You don't, for example, have control over the weather or how fit your competition is. You can, however, plan how you will deal with various weather conditions and how to pace yourself relative to other athletes. You should plan for all of the variables that are within your control.

Any plan, even a sketchy one, is better than no plan at all. The plan for a sprint-distance race may cover only a few items, whereas an Ironman-distance event plan will be quite lengthy. The section, "Example of an Ironman Race Plan," shows how detailed a plan can be.

Some athletes just discuss a plan with someone or give it a little thought. But the most effective way to plan is to write out your thoughts and objectives. I like to have the athletes I coach do this about a week before the race. By all means, share your plan with your coach, but don't just go over it verbally—put it in writing first. You could also discuss your written plan with a seasoned veteran, who may notice if you have listed something that is unreasonable or if you have overlooked something important.

Any plan, even a sketchy one, is better than no plan at all.

The race plan is already taking shape twelve weeks before the event. One week before the race, you should have a pretty good idea of what you are capable of doing. Start with your season's goal for this A-priority event. Does it still seem reasonable? Has your training gone as expected? If so, it should be easy to prepare the plan. If not, then consider

Should You Hyperhydrate?

The day before a race, it's common to see athletes walking around with bottles of water or sports drink. Is this a good idea? Does taking in a large volume of water prevent dehydration the next day? The answer is no. If you were a camel with a large reservoir designed just for holding excess water as you trudged across the desert, excessive drinking would be beneficial. But since you are reading this you are more than likely a human. We don't have a spare tank to fill. Once our limited storage areas are full, most of the excess is shunted to the bladder and removed as urine. If that's all that happened, hyperhydration would not be much of a problem. But it's not.

Excessive drinking has been shown to dilute the body's electrolyte stores, especially sodium. So excessive water intake is likely to increase your risk of hyponatremia. This is a condition in which sodium stores are too low and the body begins to shut down. In the early stages you may experience nausea, headache, muscle cramps, weakness, and disorientation. In the latter stages, seizures and coma are possible.

Although hyponatremia is unlikely to occur in races that take less than about four hours, it simply isn't a good idea to start any race, regardless of distance, with diluted electrolytes. Pay attention to your thirst mechanism. We've been taught that it is not effective and that we shouldn't trust it, but that's an old wives' tale. Drink when you are thirsty. It's that simple.

what you are realistically capable of doing in this race—either at a higher or a lower level than you originally thought possible—and create a plan that addresses the revised goal.

Of course, there could be more than one goal for a race, with some more important than others. You may have a goal to complete the race in a certain time, for example, but also have secondary goals. If something happens to prevent you from achieving the primary goal, having secondary goals can allow you to produce a worthy outcome. For example, let's say your primary goal was to finish an A-priority, Olympic-distance race in less than 2:20, but a flat tire on the bike prevented that. If you had a secondary goal of running the 10 km in a career-best 45 minutes, something positive could still be salvaged. There is no limit on secondary goals. Or you can have Plan A and Plan B. If Plan A falls out of the realm of possibility, this gives you another goal to reach for.

What should your race plan include? The following is a list of strategic variables to consider. You may not want all of these in your race plan, or you may have other important items unique to your situation that you would like to include. The variables presented below are suggested to help you get started.

Pacing. How will you control speed, effort, or power in each sport? In the swim, will you focus on going out fast in order to stay with the leaders, or will you swim at a steady pace? This decision may also help you determine where to line up at the start—front and center, to the side, or at the back. Will you watch power or heart rate on the bike? What numbers will you try to hold? How will you pace the run? Pacing is generally best based on effort, power, or heart rate—not time. External factors, such as wind, can impact time goals. Pacing is perhaps the most critical part of the plan.

Equipment. What equipment is best for this race? For the swim, consider sleeveless or full-sleeved wetsuits, or no wetsuit at all. How about wheels for the bike? How much air pressure will you put in the tires given this type of course? If the pavement is wet or there are lots of turns, consider using a lower pressure, such as 90 to 100 psi. Will you run in race flats, lightweight trainers, or your standard training shoes? How about the type of helmet, hat, or fuel belt you will use, or any other special equipment needed for the conditions of this race?

Transitions. How will you set up your transition stall, and how do you plan to flow through the transition process?

Nutrition. What will you eat or drink? How many calories will you take in and when? How much fluid? Will you take extra sodium? How much and when? Will you rely on aid stations or special-needs bags, or will you carry everything you expect to need?

Weather. What clothing and equipment changes will you need to make if there is rain, snow, or wind? What if it is unexpectedly cold, hotter than usual for the time of year, or very humid? How will you need to adjust your pacing with these unusual weather conditions?

The Sky Is Falling. Expect the unexpected and be prepared for it. How will you handle a flat tire? What if your stomach becomes upset? If this happens, what changes will you make in your eating and drinking? If this just isn't your day and things aren't going as planned, when will you decide to go to Plan B?

In the week leading up to the race, review the plan daily. You will also need a plan for how to train this week, as there is a tendency for athletes to do too much as they get closer to the race. Avoid the all-too-common urge to do one last mega-workout this week. It's too late for a major workout to help you now. If you make any mistakes, make them on the side of doing too little. And beware of goal inflation this week. Yes, you're feeling great, but that doesn't mean you've become a superhero.

Hold yourself accountable to the plan during the race. Realize that following the race, you will review how you did relative to the plan. Did you follow it? If not, why not? Frequently ask yourself what you are learning in this race that will help you do a better job of planning for the next one. If the race doesn't go as planned, it's that much more important to ask these questions and to seek constructive answers.

During the race, execute the plan, stay in the present moment, and simply do your best at all times. Take the race in little chunks. Quietly celebrate the completion of each chunk and then focus on the next—as planned. There will be good and bad patches. Stay positive in the bad patches while always moving forward. Keep the plan at the forefront of your thinking at all times.

When you must make quick decisions along the way, base your choices on your race plan, not on your emotions at the moment. If you've done your homework, you're ready. Bring it on!

EXAMPLE OF AN IRONMAN RACE PLAN

The following is an actual race plan created by Justin Daerr, one of the pro triathletes I coach.

Race week. I arrive on Tuesday late in the day. Wednesday morning I will swim at the race venue and bike afterward. Then I will head to packet pickup to register. The rest of the day is taking it easy.

Thursday is similar. I will not attend the carbo load. I'll spend this evening with my brother since he will be getting into town that day.

Friday I'll do my workouts in the morning and turn in my bike and bags. I'll keep the bags simple, no need to overpack. I may go to an early afternoon movie, see my folks afterward, and have dinner solo. They will go out that evening and I can go to sleep before they return.

Race day. Saturday (race day) I'll wake up around 3:30 a.m., drink four Ensures, and eat one bagel or a couple of pieces of toast. This comes to 1,200 to 1,300 calories. Then I'll sip water until race start, stay relaxed, and head to the race. I'll set my tire pressure to 120 psi and put everything in special-needs bags. I'll double-check the other bags, but avoid being a freak about it, and head to the beach around 6:00ish. I'll try to get a short warm-up swim in. Nothing major. Just moving some blood around.

Swim. I'll line up toward the middle inside along the front. At the gun I'll steadily move into the water and dolphin dive until the water is deep enough. Then I'll focus on long, strong strokes. I won't worry too much about everyone around me until a few hundred meters have gone by. I'm looking for a moderate start that gives me a steady sensation once I find a rhythm. Going out hard does nothing for me. I've tried it in training and I've seen the consequences. Strong and steady, looking for feet the whole time, is the key.

Transition to bike. I will get out of T1 smoothly. Bike shoes will be clipped into bike if allowed by the race director. Grab my helmet, sunglasses, two gel flasks, and race belt, get on the bike and get going.

Bike. I'll keep it comfortable to start and wait to begin racing until we turn north out of town. That should give me enough time to relax and get comfortable. I'll have two 24-ounce bottles with a combo of Endurathon and Catapult from EAS with additional sodium added. Should be around 150 calories/bottle with 100 mg of caffeine/bottle. I'll have two flasks, each with 500 calories of Hammer gel, on the bike. I'll use a sports drink from the aid stations to keep the fluids and calories up in addition to that. My special-needs bag will include two bottles identical to what I started with, but it's only there for backup.

I will try to take in close to 2,500 calories. It will be lower than that in reality, but if it's over 2,000 I think I will be just fine.

My pacing on the bike will be based on feel and reinforced by power. I will avoid extended time over 240 watts unless I need to make a move for positioning reasons. I never want to do this, but I did do it in Ironman Florida in 2003 and Kona in 2004 to get away from draft packs. I believe that racing ethically is worth the few minutes of higher power. Perhaps this won't be an issue with my improved swimming and cycling.

I will be taking splits every 5 to 10 miles and I'll be watching the average power of each. This will keep me honest. I'll soft pedal when I can and will be a bit more conservative if a tailwind is giving me 42 kph or more with lower watts. I plan to use the north winds to my advantage when they appear. Those will be good opportunities to back off and get calories in while keeping the speed high. I'll stand for 10 to 15 seconds after the aid stations to stretch a little.

Transition to run. I will be wearing the same one-piece suit for the run, so no clothes change needed. I'll put on socks and shoes, grab my water bottle, and go.

Run. The first 3 miles are easy as I take in 200+ calories from gels in this time period. After that I switch to a sports drink from the aid stations and cola for energy needs. I will take in a couple of extra gels throughout the run as I see fit—probably around miles 10 and 18.

After mile 3 I should find my effort. I'll use pace and feel to guide me and will use heart rate as reinforcement. Easy will become steady, steady will become a challenge in and of itself. Heart rate will likely be in the 155 to 165 range based on heat, fatigue, etc.

One major difference this year is that I'm putting a fuel belt in my special-needs bag. I had issues with crowded aid stations on the second loop last year so I'll be using this as backup so I won't have to completely rely on aid stations for loop 2.

My run is split into various sections. Miles 1 to 3 are easy and will revolve around getting some calories in. Then in miles 4 to 6.5 (first turnaround) I'll settle into my pace and see where I am positioned relative to the rest of the field. Miles 6.5 to 13.1 are steady as she goes. I'll get another good look at the positions of the field at this time. For miles 13.2 to 20 I really have to focus on holding pace as well as I can; if I can do that, I know I can run well relative to the field. The last 6.5 miles is the hardest part of the hardest hour of the year. I've been thinking about this hour for a long time. It's one hour, one hour that can be so rewarding if I take it one step at a time and don't back down.

I've been thinking and focusing on this race for a long time. I feel prepared and I believe in my abilities. I trust my fitness, and I'll make this one count. I know that the day could go wrong, but I will not be set back by making bad personal choices. I believe my "steady effort" is effective and competitive and I don't care where I stand until the entire race is over. The "uber" bikers can have their glory early. I'll catch them later. On the run I will be ready to make every single person work if they finish in front of me. Even if I'm racing for 20th, 19th had better be ready to race to the finish line.

Also, I know something could happen to me on the bike—flats, mechanicals, whatever. However, this is my race no matter what. If I am sidelined for an hour, I will continue to race as planned. No matter what, my goal is to run well. If that means after a six-hour bike, so be it.

I know every race has dark moments. As in life, I recognize the situation and I'll focus entirely on the task at hand. There is no such thing as a perfect day or a perfect race. Just keep moving forward. I'm excited and I'm looking forward to next weekend. This is what I love to do.

11: Recovery

Failure to take time for recovery is a training mistake. Improved fitness results not from the quantity of the exercise but from the capacity for restoration that your mind and body have. Quick recovery from fatigue is the key. This chapter discusses the phases of recovery and recovery-related problems.

THE SECRET OF RECOVERY

Athletes like Michael Phelps, who have the genetic gift of recovering quickly from workouts, seem to naturally become the best in their respective racing categories. If you weren't born with this gene, there are ways you can shorten your recovery time, and I'll discuss those later in the chapter. Although there isn't any scientific data to back this up, there does seem to be a strong correlation between one's ability to recover and the rate of one's fitness progression. Recovering quickly really means getting in good shape quickly.

Why? It's during recovery following hard training that the body realizes the changes that we call "form," which is one's potential for performance in a race or in subsequent training. These changes may result in fat-burning enzyme increases, more resilient muscles and tendons, decreases in body fat, greater heart stroke volume, better glycogen storage, and more. Besides overloading your body with the stresses of hard exercise, focusing on recovery is the most powerful thing you can do in training to perform at a higher level. But this is the part of the training process that most self-coached

TRIATHLETE'S
TRAINING BIBLE
2nd ed.

*See pp. 148–153
for more on Timing
and Technique*

athletes get wrong. They don't allow for enough recovery and overwhelm their bodies with stress.

Recovery may be thought of in many different ways. In terms of periodization, when you time recovery in your training plan and how much time you allot for it (refer to Chapters 7 and 8) will help determine your eventual success as a triathlete.

Yearly Recovery

Transition periods should follow Race periods. The purpose of these low-volume, low-intensity transitions is to allow your body and mind to rejuvenate before you begin another period of hard training. If you have two A-priority races in a season, you should also generally have two Transition periods. The first transition may only be three to five days, but the one that comes at the end of the season may well last four weeks or even longer depending on how challenging the previous season was, especially the final part.

> **Besides overloading your body with the stresses of hard exercise, focusing on recovery is the most powerful thing you can do in training to perform at a higher level.**

Monthly Recovery

Build recovery into your monthly training plan every third or fourth week. This regular period of reduced workload may be three to seven days long depending on what you did in the previous hard training weeks, how fit you are becoming, and other individual factors.

Figure 11 illustrates what happens when you do this. As your fatigue increases over the course of two to three weeks of increasing workloads, your form diminishes. Form is your potential for performance, or how well you may train or race at any given point in time. Notice that fatigue and form follow nearly opposite paths, but form lags behind the changes in fatigue. It takes a few days of reducing fatigue to produce increases in form. A key principle of training is to unload fatigue frequently, which has the effect of improving your readiness to train well again. Without unloading fatigue you become a zombie doing workouts, with low quality and no enthusiasm.

Weekly Recovery

Within each week there should be hard and easy days. No one, not even elite athletes, can train hard every day with no recovery breaks. Easy days are as

FIGURE 11: Impact of Recovery on Fatigue and Form

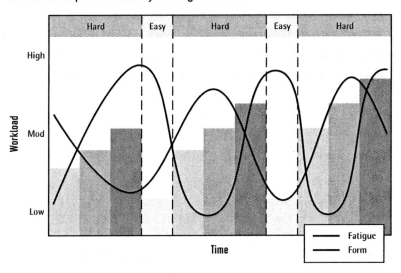

necessary for fitness and form as sleeping at night is for health and well-being. Some athletes need a day completely off from exercise every week. Other athletes, especially those with the quick-recovery gene who also have a high capacity for work, can exercise seven days a week. These elite athletes will still need easy days, however. "Easy" days are relative to the individual; there is no universal standard. That said, it is important even for high-capacity athletes to occasionally have days completely off from exercise.

Daily Recovery

When doing two-a-day workouts, there will be times when both are challenging sessions, but there will also be days when both are light workouts or one is hard and one is easy. This is what makes triathlon training so complex and why having a coach is often necessary to achieve high levels of success.

How often you insert recovery into your training program, how long this period of recovery lasts, and what exactly recovery means to you in terms of workout duration, intensity, and frequency are an individual matter. The only sure way for you to determine each of these is trial and error. Some athletes will find they can recover quite nicely in short periods of infrequent recovery. Others will discover they need frequent long periods to recover adequately.

Be aware that the need for recovery is a moving target; it is always changing in response to the total stress in your life and how fit you are.

Be conservative when trying different recovery programs. "Conservative" in this case means erring on the side of too much recovery.

RECOVERY-RELATED PROBLEMS

With rare exceptions, the setbacks we experience in training are of our own making. Our motivation to excel is exceeded only by our inability to listen to our bodies. The result is often overtraining, illness, or injury.

Overtraining

Athletes often ask me to review their training logs to see what might be behind a recent poor performance. What I usually find is that the athlete has been neglecting recovery and needs a few days of rest. I seldom find athletes who are really overtrained. Fatigue generally prevents athletes from driving themselves into a full-blown overtrained state. But I do find such athletes on occasion. The most common cause is an overwhelming motivation to excel.

A few years ago, a self-coached pro triathlete called me to ask if I could review his log because his race performances were declining. I arranged to meet him to learn more. When we met, I didn't have to read his log to know what the problem was. Sitting in front of me was a lackluster young man with a slumped posture and bags under his eyes who spoke in a monotone. He told me he wasn't sleeping well at night and that he had to drag himself out of bed in the morning to train.

He said he had skipped a couple of recovery periods, as he was racing so well in the spring that he figured he didn't need them. And with the most important races of the season just around the corner, he decided he could cram in more hard workouts by skipping the rest breaks. This "Superman Syndrome" is common when fitness is high. But when some "Kryptonite" appeared, he tried training harder than before to overcome the downward spiral. That made things even worse. He couldn't reverse the loss of fitness no matter what he did with his workouts. So in frustration, he called me.

I told him exactly what he didn't want to hear but what he suspected deep down was at the heart of the flagging performance—he was overtrained. I had never seen an athlete in such a run-down state. There was only one cure: He had to rest. I advised him to take a complete break from training. I wasn't sure how long it would take—it could be days until he came around, or it could be months—but I suspected it would take a longer time rather than a shorter one for him to recover.

He took a week off and then did a short, easy bike ride. His power was low and his perceived exertion was high. But more telling was that he still experienced deep fatigue, and his enthusiasm for life in general was low. So he took another week off. After a couple of weeks of rest he started to have more energy and desire to train, so I had him gradually return to something approaching normal training. It was still a long way from what he had been doing before all of this started. But at least he was back on the road to racing again.

I was his coach for the next two years until his retirement from professional sports. In that time he won several more big races. He frequently told me that he was never again the same athlete after that overtraining episode. He couldn't train with the volume and intensity he had previously found easy. He believed something about his physiology had changed that spring. He may well have been right. There is still a great deal to be learned about overtraining. It could be that overtraining causes hormonal dysfunction that results in irreversible disturbances in glandular function. We simply don't know.

The bottom line is that you must avoid overtraining at all costs. In just a few weeks you can flood your body with stress hormones that may have a long-lasting and debilitating effect. If you make a mistake in coaching yourself, make it on the side of doing too little rather than too much.

TRIATHLETE'S
TRAINING BIBLE
2nd ed.

See pp. 141–144
for more on
Overtraining

12: Skills

As described in *The Triathlete's Training Bible*, when you improve the basic abilities of endurance, force, and speed skills, and the more advanced abilities of muscular endurance, anaerobic endurance, and power, you will realize your goal of greater race velocity. Another way of looking at the necessary fitness components uses the terms of science: Great race fitness results from a large aerobic capacity (VO_2max), a high lactate threshold as a percentage of aerobic capacity, and an excellent economy of movement. Although you may not be as familiar with economy as you are with the concepts of aerobic capacity and lactate threshold, it is critical for you to understand how improving economy can help you achieve greater gains.

EQUIPMENT TO IMPROVE SWIM ECONOMY

Swimming has many more tools and toys than the other two triathlon sports do. And they really can help you become a better swimmer. But you've got to be a bit cautious with swim aids—they can be addictive. Use them only when you are working on refining technique, not for every set in every swim session.

Fins. The slower you go while swimming, the more likely you are to sink. Your hips and legs are especially prone to sinking, which increases drag. Using fins eliminates this problem because they promote greater propulsion, allowing you to focus on form while staying high in the water. Look for the short, stubby fins rather than the long type used by divers.

Snorkel. Poor technique, not aerobic fitness, is the primary limiter for most triathletes when it comes to swimming. And the number one contributor to poor technique is inefficient breathing. The need to breathe frequently gets in the way for athletes trying to perfect body position and arm and leg synchronization. One of the best tools to help with this challenge is a snorkel. It allows you to concentrate on getting body mechanics right without constantly turning to get air. Once you've learned correct arm and body technique, the breathing technique is easily incorporated.

Paddles. There are two basic types of hand paddles. The large, flat, squarish ones are designed primarily to help you improve upper-body strength. They increase the resistance that your hand, arm, and upper body must overcome to move you through the water. As your strength improves, your economy also improves. The other type of paddle is more sleek-looking and may have a small "keel" sticking out on the bottom. These are intended to help you refine your hand and arm position at water entry by encouraging a high elbow during the catch-and-pull phase of your stroke. But you do not have to purchase both types. If you wear the square type by only using the finger loop and not the wrist strap, it will have the same effect of encouraging correct hand placement.

Cadence meter. Once you have learned proper technique, you will want to focus on improving your stroke rate (cadence) and your stroke distance. Good freestyle endurance swimmers typically have a stroke rate of about 40 to 55 cycles per minute. One cycle is the time it takes from one right-hand entry to the next right-hand entry. Getting closer to this cadence will help you become more efficient. Using a small cadence meter worn in your swim cap or clipped onto your goggle strap will make you more aware of stroke rate and distance per stroke. It emits an audible beep that can be adjusted to various rates.

TRIATHLETE'S
TRAINING BIBLE
2nd ed.

See pp. 159–165
for more on
Swim Skills

GROUP SWIMMING: A CASE STUDY

I began working with Marlene when she was 43 years old and a strong cyclist. My plan was to help her maintain her bike fitness while emphasizing swimming and running. I thought her running would come along well, as she had a big aerobic engine. But swimming was a different story. She did not have any experience with competitive swimming. She was, however, a golfer and so could relate to a sport primarily based on skill rather than fitness, at least in the initial stages of development.

The first week I coached Marlene I had her do the "T1" workout described in Appendix B of the *Training Bible*. This is an interval test set in which she completed ten 100 meter swims as fast as she could go, with 10-second recovery breaks between efforts. Her average pace for the 100s was 1:57. She wanted to markedly increase her time.

Over the next ten months, Marlene swam by herself with an emphasis on technique, and her average 100 meter time for T1 steadily came down until it reached 1:45—a 10 percent improvement, or about 1 percent per month. Not bad. At about this time she found a masters swim group that had a coach on deck. She also began meeting with the swim coach for underwater video recording and technique instruction. Over the next three months, her T1 test time dropped to 1:34. That was an 11 percent gain, or nearly 4 percent per month.

If you want to become a faster swimmer, having other swimmers in the pool with you doing the same workouts makes a big difference.

I've had this same experience with every swimming-challenged triathlete I've ever coached. I don't usually recommend group workouts for cycling or running, but with swimming I've found that they can be beneficial. There is little change in performance when an athlete swims alone, or in the absence of instruction on proper technique. But test and race times start dropping once either group swims or an instructor is added into the mix. If you want to become a faster swimmer, having other swimmers in the pool with you doing the same workouts makes a big difference. So does having an experienced coach on deck giving you feedback on technique. Finally, seeing your stroke on video and learning how to change it makes you more aware of proper technique and hastens the learning process. This is a sure way to become a better swimmer.

IMPROVING CYCLING ECONOMY

Pedaling Cadence

Economy in riding a bike is based on an interaction between a human and a machine. How well they fit together is a significant determining factor in cadence economy. For example, short crank arms favor pedaling at a high cadence, and a high saddle position slows the cadence.

In triathlon, the cadence you use determines not only how you feel on the bike but also how your legs will feel in the ensuing run. Low cadences put stress on the knees and muscles and require greater muscular force generation than high cadences. High cadences require great metabolic effort, which causes heavy breathing, for example. This means that a high cadence minimizes muscle fatigue but may cause you to use more energy, at least until you are adapted to it.

Observations of elite riders in triathlons reveal a common cadence range of about 80 to 100 rpm. This range is also supported by research. Studies dating back to 1913 have shown the most economical cadence to vary from 33 to 110 rpm. More sophisticated recent studies, however, have tended to favor higher cadences, at least when they are self-selected by accomplished riders.

It is also interesting to compare the cadences used by elite triathletes in races of different lengths. Cadence tends to be low in Ironman-distance races—often around 80 rpm—while in sprint-distance races it is more likely to be in the high 90s.

The bottom line is that it appears that once your bike is set up correctly, pedaling at a cadence in the range of 80 to 100 rpm on a flat course is probably best. Increasing the range of your comfortable cadences ultimately produces a broader range of efficiency. That will give you greater economy even if you race in long events at low cadences such as 80 rpm.

Cornering Skills

Another critical cycling skill is cornering, which is a safety and a performance issue. The most common cause of crashes is poor cornering skills. Improving your cornering skills can also save you a significant amount of time on a course with lots of turns.

As you can see in Figure 12, there are three ways to handle your bike when cornering—leaning, countersteering, and steering.

Leaning method. The leaning method is the most common cornering technique in triathlon regardless of the cornering situation. But it is really best when it is necessary to make a wide, sweeping turn on dry, clean pavement. In the United States and other countries where drivers and cyclists ride on the right side of the road, it is most effective when turning left. For those countries where drivers and cyclists stay on the left, this is the preferred right-turn method. To use the method, simply lean both the bike and

FIGURE 12: Bicycle Cornering Techniques

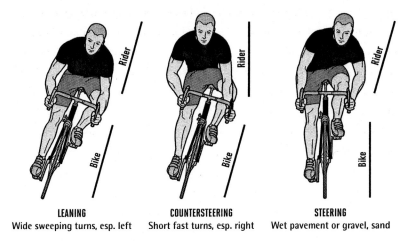

LEANING	COUNTERSTEERING	STEERING
Wide sweeping turns, esp. left	Short fast turns, esp. right	Wet pavement or gravel, sand

your body into the turn with your weight on the outside pedal. If it is truly a wide, sweeping turn, you may be able to remain in the aero position and continue pedaling.

Countersteering method. Few triathletes use the countersteering technique, but it is quite effective for tight turns, such as right-hand turns in ride-on-the-right countries and left-hand turns in ride-on-the-left countries. Countersteering will get you around the corner with a much tighter radius than the leaning method will, saving you time.

If you've learned countersteering on a motorcycle, the technique is the same. You must stop pedaling as you enter the turn because the bike tilt will be greater than with the leaning method. The inside pedal is up and your body weight is fully on the outside pedal. Here's where it feels counterintuitive: Straighten your arm on the inside of the turn and bend the elbow on the outside of the turn. It seems backwards, as you're pushing on the opposite handlebar you would use for a sweeping turn. This motion breaks the gyroscopic effect of the turning wheels and causes you to lean the bike sharply into the turn as your body stays upright. You will go around the corner on a tight radius. In order for this technique to be effective, your speed must be at least 15 mph (24 kph) or so. It takes practice to make it habitual.

Steering method. Use this method when cornering on wet pavement or when there is sand or gravel on the road surface. Regardless of whether this is a right or left turn, you will need to slow down. If it is a tight-radius turn, such as a right turn in the United States, you must also stop pedaling.

The purpose is to get around the corner safely without falling. The proper method involves keeping the bike upright while leaning only your body into the turn. Keep both knees near the top tube of the bike—do not point your knee at the corner.

Other cornering considerations. When riding on wet pavement, reduce your tire pressure by about 25 percent. This will give you better traction on the corners and help prevent a crash while having minimal effect on overall speed. The type of tire you use also plays a role when cornering. Tubular tires, also called "sew-ups," corner better than clinchers, as they have round sidewalls, whereas clinchers have straighter sidewalls. Be especially careful when cornering on wet pavement if there is a painted stripe on the road. When wet, these are like ice. Use extreme caution when cornering on wet pavement in steep descents. Apply your brakes well before you get to the corner to reduce speed. Do not use the brakes when cornering.

TRIATHLETE'S
TRAINING BIBLE
2nd ed.

*See pp. 165–170
for more on
Bike Skills*

EQUIPMENT TO IMPROVE CYCLING ECONOMY

The bike portion of a triathlon usually accounts for about half of your race finish time. So improving economy on the bike has the most potential of the three sports to reduce your race times. You can use a variety of equipment to increase your economy.

Rollers. Most triathletes, especially those in northern states, have an indoor trainer of some sort for those winter days when it's too dark and nasty to ride outside. Indoor trainers usually lock the rear wheel of your bike in place against a resistance-generating device. Another type of trainer, less commonly used, consists of freely turning rollers in both front and back that you set your bike on. Since the bike is not locked in place, you balance it while riding just as you do outdoors.

The disadvantage of rollers is that it is more challenging to do certain techniques, like single-leg drills. The advantage is that you can work on pedaling skills in a more realistic condition with the bike moving beneath you, just as it does on the road. This makes working on pedaling skills more effective. But rollers take some getting used to. The first few times you ride on rollers, put the device in a doorway to keep from coming off the side and slamming into a wall.

Power Cranks. The single-leg training described earlier is one of the best drills for improving bike-pedaling skills. With "Power Cranks"™— unconnected crank arms that move independently of each other—you can work on individual leg skills without having to unclip from the pedals. This allows you to pedal with one leg while the other is not moving, as in single-leg drills.

When you are pedaling normally with Power Cranks, each leg is working in isolation from the other leg. This allows you to discover your pedaling weaknesses and focus on them. What too often happens with standard cranks is that the recovery leg on the upstroke side rests on the pedal, forcing the leg on the downstroke side to work harder to lift the lazy recovery leg. This wastes a tremendous amount of energy, which reduces your economy. But your legs cannot get lazy when using Power Cranks.

I'd recommend putting Power Cranks on a second bicycle rather than your primary bike so you don't have to change cranks every time you want to use them. Riding with them two to four times each week in the Base period will do wonders for your pedaling skills. Then ride them once or twice weekly year round to maintain skills. You'll probably find when first starting to use Power Cranks that short rides are best. To find out more, go to Powercranks.com.

Fixed-gear bike. As mentioned above, a fixed-gear bike is a bike that has only one gear. It has no derailleurs and won't allow you to coast without pedaling. Whenever the wheels are turning, the cranks are also turning. The typical fixed-gear bike is also usually set up with a low gearing combination that keeps the rider at a fairly high cadence, such as 110 to 120 rpm. And since high cadences encourage the improvement of pedaling skills, the fixed-gear bike is a great tool.

As with Power Cranks, it's best to set up a second bike with a fixed gear. For more information on fixed-gear bikes and to learn how to convert one of your old bikes, go to Sheldonbrown.com/fixed.html.

Q-Rings. Another worthwhile product is the oval-shaped chainrings that replace the standard chainrings on your bike. Q-Rings are especially good for triathletes who tend to "mash" the pedals rather than spin the cranks smoothly. When your pedal is at the top and bottom of the stroke, the Q-Ring is in the smallest-radius position (the pointy ends of the oval are parallel to the crank), which means your foot can more easily make the transition. When in the power position at 3 o'clock, the radius is at its greatest length, which gives you more leverage and therefore more power. For example, a 53-tooth Q-Ring is the equivalent of pedaling with a 51 tooth at the top and bottom and a 56 tooth at 3 o'clock. You can find out more about Q-Rings at Rotorcranksusa.com.

Midsole cleat. Most of the triathletes I coach have found that moving their cleats from the traditional ball-of-the-foot position to the arch of their shoes has improved their economy. And even better, when the cleat is in this position the amount of work done by the calf muscles while pedaling is significantly reduced. That means that the calf muscles, the primary running muscles, are fresher coming off the bike. Such double benefits are hard to come by.

It's not easy to find shoes with midsole cleats. You can have them custom made or you can convert existing shoes. Your local bike shop should be able to help. Not all cycling shoes will accommodate an arch-mounted cleat. If yours will, use an old pair of shoes initially to see whether or not you like this cleat position. You may also have to change your pedal system because slightly cupped cleats won't fit on flat arch areas. You could try a mountain-bike cleat, which generally has only two bolts and will fit snugly on a flat shoe arch area.

If you are unwilling to make such a radical change, try simply moving your cleats as far back toward the heel as your shoe and cleat will allow. This may only be a quarter of an inch, but that will still reduce some of the work your calf muscles must do.

IMPROVING RUNNING ECONOMY

Running Posture

Chin on chest, shoulders slumped and sagging, back humped and bent at the waist, arms nearly straight or held high in front of the chest crossing the body midline with every step—these are some of the postural energy wasters seen all too often in age-group runners. Poor posture contributes to slow running times because it forces the body to rely strictly on the legs for propulsion. Running is a total-body activity that demands good form and core strength for efficiency and effectiveness.

Improving your running posture is the first step to improving your performance. One way to check your posture is to have someone shoot a video of you from both the front and side as you run. Then take your camera to a race and record some of the top runners during their warm-ups, or in the race itself, if you're there as a spectator. Watch the movies and compare your technique with theirs. It's likely you will see significant postural differences along the lines of the flaws listed above.

Decide what needs to be changed and go to work on it. It will take several weeks of frequently checking your posture during runs to see if your flaws are under control before the new positioning finally becomes a good habit. You can use video or ask a friend to check your form as you continue to develop positional awareness. Bad form is most likely to appear when you are tired or under mental stress.

Running Cadence

Many triathletes try to get faster by maximizing stride length with a slow cadence. To get this long stride they have to raise their center of gravity by a few inches with every step, bouncing as they run. This "loping" stride has several implications.

The first is that the runner needlessly expends a lot of extra energy. Remember, in a race, the finish line is in a horizontal direction, not a vertical one. The second implication is that once he or she is up in the air, the loping runner is dependent on gravity for a return to earth. On this planet, all objects, including human bodies, fall at the same increasing velocity—32 feet per second per second. Vertical displacement means slower running due to the time spent falling back to the ground. The third implication of loping is that when the runner does come back to terra firma, there is a considerable impact force. Repeating this a few hundred times each mile, mile after mile, year after year, often results in the overuse injuries that plague runners.

So the way to run faster is not with a longer stride, at least not when you are initially trying to improve your running, but rather with a quicker cadence. Increasing your cadence will minimize your vertical displacement, allowing you more frequent contacts with the ground, which is when horizontal power is applied, and will decrease your risk of injury because you will experience a lighter landing.

The next time you watch a race having world-class runners, count their right-foot steps for 20 seconds. Even toward the end of a marathon you'll almost always find that they take 30 or more right-foot steps—that's a cadence of at least 90 rpm. Even when they are running slowly, you'll find their cadence is relatively high. They aren't loping along at 80 rpm. That makes them very economical.

The Kenyan runners set a great example. Their cadence is typically 96, plus or minus 2, and in any given triathlon or marathon, the Kenyans are usually the ones with the highest cadences in the lead group. They are also among the most economical runners in the world, owing in large part to their high cadences. We could learn a lot from them when it comes to improving our own running economy.

Minimal Support Time

The main limiter for velocity in running has to do with how much force is applied to the ground in a brief instant. As the foot strikes the pavement, it applies a force, and since, according to Isaac Newton, for every applied force there is an equal and opposite reactive force, your body moves up and forward. The distance you move forward (stride length) is partly determined by how quickly the force was applied. Time is a major component of power. As time in contact with the ground decreases, power increases. If, when your running shoe comes in contact with the road, you linger for just a split second too long, the applied power drops, which shortens your stride. You run slower, even though you have now increased your cadence. The idea is to spend very little time with your feet planted on the ground.

It really doesn't take much of a change to speed up your running pace considerably. For example, one study found that runners who learned to keep their feet on the ground only 15 milliseconds (0.015 second) less than their previous average—that is, decreasing the time by about the length of an eye blink—ran 3 percent faster. By making the same small improvement, a runner doing a 10 km in 40 minutes could shave off more than a minute, and a 4-hour marathon would speed up by 7 minutes. Those are pretty significant time savings, and they are achieved without months of suffering through intervals, hill work, and high mileage.

One study found that runners who learned to keep their feet on the ground only 15 milliseconds less than their previous average ran 3 percent faster.

To decrease ground contact time, you have to change the way your foot initially lands with each stride. There are three ways your foot can strike the ground. You can land on your heel, the ball of your foot, or midfoot with a simultaneous heel and ball landing. Let's examine each.

Heel landing. Most slow runners use a heel landing. Just before the foot strikes the ground, the knee is extended with the foot leading and the toes pointing up. It's exactly the same thing you would do if you were trying to stop. Once the heel comes in contact with the ground with the toes in the air, the only way to get off the foot again is to roll forward from heel to toe like a rocking chair. That takes a lot of time, and it requires a considerable amount of power to reaccelerate from braking.

To make matters worse, this kind of landing transmits a lot of shock up the leg, since the heel bone is not designed to absorb such impact forces. The risk of injury to the leg bones, ankle, knee, hip, and lower back is increased.

This is not an effective way to run, and yet it is by far the most prevalent landing style among age-group triathletes, primarily because of shoes. We were not meant to run in them—hunter-gatherers certainly didn't—but we are forced to by the hard surfaces we typically run on. The thick heel pad of your shoe encourages you to land on it. Pay attention the next time you run barefoot. Notice that you don't land on your heels.

Forefoot landing. Most elite runners land on the forefoot. When they do this, the foot looks to be almost flat to the ground, but their heels are unweighted. The runner bends the knee an instant before landing with the foot directly below it and parallel to the horizon. The foot "paws back" just a bit before contacting the ground. Actually, it doesn't move backward, it decelerates. Relative to the knee, the foot is moving backward. Relative to a camera looking up from the road surface, the foot is moving forward but slowing down slightly just before landing. At landing, the fast runner's body weight goes immediately to the forefoot and starts to toe off. It is more like a rocking chair than a pogo stick—the foot quickly comes off the road without braking.

The forefoot is designed to absorb shock. There are 26 bones in the foot held together by various sinews. When you land on the forefoot, most of these bones spread out laterally, absorbing shock much the same way the shock absorbers on your car do. Your risk of injury to bone and joints is decreased.

I would not recommend, however, that you try this if you are currently a heel striker, for although the risk of injury to bones and joints decreases, the potential for injury to the plantar fascia, Achilles tendon, and calf increases. Elite runners who do this have adapted to it over many years, usually decades. But as a longtime heel striker, you may find that your legs aren't ready for a sudden change. Instead, make the change to a midfoot landing.

Midfoot landing. With a midfoot landing, both the heel and the ball of the foot come in contact with the ground at the same time, with body weight fairly evenly distributed between the forefoot and the heel. Just before foot strike the knee is slightly bent, with the foot directly below it, and the foot paws back as in the forefoot landing. Again, be aware that the foot is not actually moving backward from the perspective of the road. But viewed from the knee it is moving backward.

At first you may find that you must breathe more heavily, that you feel like you are working harder, and that you are slower with a midfoot landing than with a heel landing. That's because your body is being forced to adapt to something it isn't used to. Start by doing only six to eight 20-second intervals on grass two or three times each week for a month while concentrating on the paw-back technique. After a month you should be starting to get the hang of it. Then start incorporating the technique into your shortest runs. After a

FIGURE 13: Efficient Running Form

month of this you should be ready to do all of your running with a midfoot landing. Be patient and stick with it. You'll soon run faster than ever.

Figure 13 shows how a midfoot strike looks. Essentially, it minimizes the time your foot spends on the ground and enhances the rebound effect while keeping the brakes off. If you are now a well-established heel striker, try to make slow and steady progress toward changing your landing form. Don't try to go too quickly, as landing farther forward on the foot places new stresses on the feet and lower legs that could result in an injury. Save this change for the next Prep period of the training year when run durations are short. At first run only on soft surfaces, such as grass, dirt, or a track, allowing plenty of time for recovery between runs.

EQUIPMENT TO IMPROVE RUNNING ECONOMY

Breaking old habits can be difficult, and nowhere is this more true than in running. If you have been running for a number of years, adopting the quick cadence and midfoot landing described earlier will be a challenge. The following equipment can help you.

Shoes. The shoes you run in have a lot to do with how economical you are. When buying shoes, always shop at a store that specializes in running equipment, especially if you tend to experience frequent running injuries or need to make changes in your running form. Running shoes are very individualized. The wrong ones can interfere with running mechanics and cause injury. Shoe selection is made all the more challenging by the overwhelming number of constantly changing options on the market.

Be wary of running shoes with thick heels. These will make it hard for you to learn to run with a proper foot landing. The higher your heel, the more side-to-side movements your foot will make while running, which is likely to set you up for an injury. Those who may need higher heels are people prone to plantar fascia, Achilles tendon, or calf injuries.

You will find many shoes designed to help control excessive pronation. This is because many runners find that their feet flatten out and roll too much to the inside on contact with the road. Interestingly, the higher the heel of the shoe is, the more likely you are to need some sort of pronation-reducing device built into the shoe. Refer to an experienced running-shoe salesperson to help decide whether or not you need pronation-controlling shoes. Bring your worn-out shoes with you so that the salesperson can examine the pattern of wear; this can provide important clues about the style of shoes that will work best for you.

As a general rule, look for the "least shoe" possible. On one hand, if you are small and lean, have a perfect foot strike and high cadence, are light on your feet, run only on soft surfaces, and have no history of injuries, you can use a lightweight trainer or perhaps even a racing shoe. On the other hand, if you are a 200-pounder, land on your heels, run on concrete, excessively pronate, and have experienced several running injuries, you will need a much more substantial shoe. **As a general rule, look for the "least shoe" possible.** You will probably find that you land somewhere between these two extremes. But don't make a drastic change to a minimalist shoe even if you're convinced it is right for you. Buy a slightly different design and alternate the new shoe with your old ones to allow your body time to adapt over a few weeks. After six weeks or so, consider purchasing an even less restrictive shoe and alternating that with the other pair you most recently bought. Getting into the right shoes could take you several months and costs money. Be patient.

Cadence meter. Having a device with an audible tone that you can set for various cadences can help you increase your cadence in running just as in swimming with counting strokes. In fact, you can use the same device you use for swimming by fastening it to a running cap. Some watches also have a metronome feature. Or you can buy a small, electronic metronome at a music store and carry it in a pocket. Again, don't try to make the change from a low cadence to a high cadence overnight. This will take several weeks, if not several months, of slight increases that gradually build up to a significant change.

Movie camera. There is no better way to improve your form than to have visual evidence of exactly how you run. In this regard, a movie camera is one of the best tools available for monitoring your progression.

Have someone record you running both in side view and as you run toward the camera. In the side view, look to see how you are doing in regard to the key features of economical running—you should be leaning slightly forward from the ankle, with your foot below the knee just before foot strike, and you should land with the entire foot coming in contact with the road at the same instant rather than heel first. You should be able to draw an imaginary straight line from your ear through the hip and to the support foot. When examining the front view, check whether or not you can see the black bottom of the shoe before landing. If so, you are landing on the heel. Also check that you aren't swaying from side to side.

Take new videos weekly and compare them with the previous ones to gauge your progression and to see what areas you still need to focus on. Doing this will speed up the learning process and make you a more economical runner sooner than if you just went by the observations of others or by how you felt you were doing. You will be amazed at the continual improvement.

TRIATHLETE'S
TRAINING BIBLE
2nd ed.

*See pp. 170–177
for more on
Run Skills*

13: Muscles

In the *Training Bible*, I outlined an approach to strength training and stretching to complement your training and make your time in the gym more purposeful and effective. The regimen outlined in Chapter 13 of the Training Bible will strengthen the muscle groups you rely on for swimming, cycling, and running, ultimately improving your endurance and building resistance against injury. In addition to improving endurance, your strength training can improve your speed skills and force. The exercises and programs that follow should help you tailor your strength training to your needs, and enhance your triathlon performance considerably.

SUPPLEMENTAL FUNCTIONAL EXERCISE

Becoming stronger while maintaining or improving the range of motion of your joints will help you perform more efficiently and powerfully while preventing injury. But stability, muscular coordination, and muscular balance are also important for muscular performance. Exercises that supplement your primary sports training can do a great deal to improve your triathlon efficiency and power while also preventing many of the problems that develop when muscles are subject to repetitive motions and overuse. You will be doing most of these supplemental exercises in a gym, but you can build some of them into your swim, bike, and run workouts, especially during the warm-ups or cool-downs. They will complement the movements of the three sports.

Stability on the Bike

Stability means that you can maintain a position or posture, especially when on an unstable surface. You're certainly familiar with learning to balance a bike as a child. Becoming skilled at this was no small feat, as the surface you were on, two tires with minimal road contact, is really unstable. Many triathletes still have poor balance skills when cornering or avoiding obstacles in the road, especially when riding slowly, as is often required by poor road conditions.

The slalom and bottle-pickup drills are great for triathletes with poor bike balance skills. To do the slalom drill, set up a half-dozen water bottles or other soft placeholders in a parking lot. Put them in a straight line about 15 feet apart. As you ride the slalom course, weave around the bottles on alternate sides—go left of the first one, right of the second, left of the third, and so on. Ride with your hands on the bars, not in the aero position. Practice good cornering skills by placing the outside pedal (left pedal when making a right turn) down with your weight on it. Lean the bike into the turn by countersteering with your inside arm straight and the outside arm bent (see Figure 12 in *Companion* Chapter 12). The faster you go, the more you will lean the bike into the turn. As you get better, move the bottles closer together. Make it a game by timing yourself and doing it with a training partner to see who can negotiate the course faster.

The bottle-pickup drill is just as it sounds. Place a water bottle upright in a parking lot and ride past it while reaching down to pick it up. Try it on both sides. When you have mastered this drill, repeat it with the bottle on its side, so you have to reach down farther to pick it up. Such drills will improve your ability to balance your bike and make you a more accomplished cyclist.

Stability on the Run

Running requires excellent balance, but we usually don't think about it because it seems to come naturally.

Your foot provides little real stability; it is posture and balance that keep you vertical. When you are in midstride with one foot on the ground, you are essentially balancing on a small tripod. The inner and outer edges of the ball of your foot make up two of the support points; the third support point is your heel. In midfoot-strike distance running, all three of the support points are very briefly in contact with the ground at the same time. In order to maintain balance for that split second, hundreds of muscles are activated in a coordinated effort throughout your entire body. The better the nervous system is at firing these muscles in the most efficient way, the less effort it takes to run. If balance is poor, you will waste a lot of energy without even being aware of it. The less energy you waste, the faster and farther you run.

The best way to improve balance is to repeatedly challenge yourself with balancing drills. For example, stand on one foot with a bent-knee running posture and play catch with a friend. Try not to touch your raised foot to the ground for as many catches and throws as possible. To make it even more challenging, stand on an unstable surface such as a soft rubber pad, wobble board, or BOSU ball. You may even do some light weight lifting while standing on one leg or on an unstable surface. Challenge your balance frequently in the early Base period and then less frequently, but regularly, in the Build period.

One word of caution is necessary here. Do not attempt the heavy weight training suggested in the *Training Bible* while standing on unstable surfaces. Not only is it dangerous, it is also an ineffective way to develop maximal, sport-specific strength. When attempting weight training, always do the exercises on stable floors and equipment.

Muscular Coordination

When we say someone has "good coordination," we mean that his or her movements have a certain smoothness and grace. "Muscular coordination" simply refers to the ability to time the contractions and relaxations of all the muscles involved in a smooth movement. For swimming, biking, and running, most of the body's muscles must be innervated and relaxed in an intricate pattern.

Most of the strength exercises in Chapter 13 of the *Training Bible* involve two or more joints bending and straightening in a coordinated way. That is because single-joint exercises, such as a knee extension, do little to improve the intricate muscle-firing patterns necessary for sport performance. Multijoint

Exercises that supplement your primary sports training can do a great deal to improve your triathlon efficiency and power while also preventing many of the problems that develop when muscles are subject to repetitive motions and overuse.

exercises, such as a squat, involve muscle-firing patterns that more closely approximate the movements of running and pedaling. The role of single-joint exercises for the triathlete is to improve the strength of a muscle group that is unusually weak and susceptible to injury.

Age-group triathletes, especially masters, tend to have poor coordination because, like most people, they initially learned to swim, bike, and run with poor skills and inappropriate muscle-firing patterns. These patterns were thoroughly ingrained over several years of training. Breaking longtime patterns can be a difficult challenge.

The starting point for changing poor skills and bad habits is awareness. Until you are aware of where your hand enters the water, where your knee is at the top of the pedal stroke, or where your recovery foot is when running, you will never be able to improve them. Pay close attention to body positions when working out, using video or even mirrors to observe your movements when possible.

The drills mentioned in Chapter 12 of both the *Companion* and the *Training Bible* will help train your muscles to fire and relax at the right times, but only if you pay attention to where your head, shoulders, arms, knees, feet, and various other body parts are throughout the drills. Doing them without paying close attention and making small, almost imperceptible, corrections is a waste of your time.

Muscular Balance

Because swimming, biking, and running all involve straightforward, repetitive movements, it is possible for the human body to make exceptional muscular and nervous system adaptations to perform them economically and efficiently. Through several years of training, the serious triathlete becomes very good at them. But for the same reason, they can also be detrimental as a result of the imbalances and postural changes that can occur. The most likely downside is injury when the forward-moving muscles are overdeveloped and the lateral ones all but ignored.

To improve muscular balance for swimming, include other strokes in workouts, especially in the warm-up and cool-down. The backstroke, flystroke, and breaststroke will help correct muscular imbalances caused by doing only freestyle swimming.

Overcoming muscular imbalances due to cycling is difficult since you can't change your position on your bike very much, or the single-plane movements of your feet while attached to the pedals. But in the weight room you may include some lateral strength building exercises, such as side lunges, side step-ups onto a box, and leg abduction and adduction exercises, to help balance out your muscular development.

One exercise I often have runners do is called "carioca." This is great for improving the strength of the lateral muscles of the hip, especially the gluteus medius. This is a small muscle in your hip that is about where the outer seam of the rear pocket of your jeans is located. I've yet to find a serious runner with strong glute meds. Weakness in this muscle causes the athlete to rely more heavily on the tensor fascia latae (TFL) muscles on the side of the hip. As the TFLs become overdeveloped, excess tension is placed on the iliotibial band running down the outside of the thigh, which often results in lateral knee pain. This is one of the most prevalent injuries in runners and also one of the slowest to heal.

To do the carioca, simply run sideways to the right by crossing the left leg behind the right on step 1, then the left leg in front of the right leg on step 2, left behind right for step 3, and so on. Run for 20 seconds or so like this and then run to the left, reversing the leg-crossover pattern. This is a great exercise to include in your warm-up and will give you much greater lateral hip strength and hip mobility.

Seasonal Periodization of Strength Training

Strength training with weights needs to dovetail with your triathlon-specific training so that the two modes are complementary. If they don't mesh well, then you may find that you are tired frequently and that your swim, bike, and run training isn't progressing. Table 4 shows you when to do each phase of strength training during your annual season.

TRIATHLETE'S
TRAINING BIBLE
2nd ed.

See pp. 183-188 for more on Strength Phases and Periodization

If you have two or more Race periods in a season, it is recommended that you return to the Maximum Strength (MS) phase whenever you repeat the Base period, even if it is just for 4 to 6 sessions before you return to Strength Maintenance (SM). Should you have a periodization plan with only one Race period, which generally is not a good idea but is sometimes done, return to MS (or daily undulating workouts) for 4 to 6 sessions about every 16 weeks. The challenge when doing this is that your swim, bike, and run training may decline when you are lifting heavy loads. You will need to allow for this by reducing the intensity of triathlon-specific workouts, especially the

TABLE 4: Periodization of Strength Training

PERIOD	STRENGTH PHASE
Prep	AA-MT
Base 1	MS
Base 2	SM
Base 3	SM
Build 1	SM
Build 2	SM
Peak	SM
Race	(None)

day after a strength session. In essence, you would be inserting mini–Base periods every 16 weeks and emphasizing duration at these times.

Daily Undulating Strength Phase

Total sessions/phase	12–18
Sessions/week	2–3
Load (% 1RM)	Build with each set
Sets/session	2–3
Reps/set*	Set 1: 15 Set 2: 10 Set 3: 5
Speed of lift*	Slow to moderate
Recovery (in minutes)*	2–4

*Note: Only boldfaced exercises below follow this guideline. All others continue AA guidelines.

EXERCISES
(in order of completion):

1.   **Hip extension (squat, leg press, or step-up)**
2.   **Seated row**
3.   Abdominal with twist
4.   Upper-body choice (chest press or lat pull-down)
5.   Personal weakness (hamstring curl, knee extension, or heel raise)
6.   Standing row

LOAD GOALS BASED ON BODY WEIGHT (BW)

Freebar squat   1.3–1.7 x BW

Leg press (sled) 2.5–2.9 x BW

Step-up   0.7–0.9 x BW

Seated row   0.5–0.8 x BW

Standing row   0.4–0.7 x BW

TRIATHLETE'S
TRAINING BIBLE
2nd ed.

*See pp. 188–198
for Strength
Exercises*

Undulating Periodization of Strength Training

The linear strength training periodization model explained in this chapter corresponds to the classic or linear training model described in Chapter 3. That chapter also mentioned another model, "daily undulating" periodization, which can also be beneficial.

Undulating periodization is a simple scheme to follow daily. During the six weeks or so devoted to the Maximum Transition (MT) and MS phases in the linear model, you do both MT and MS in a combined workout for each weight-lifting exercise in each workout. If, for example, you are doing three sets, you would do the first set with a load that you could lift only about 15 times. You would do the second set with a load you could lift 10 times, and the third set with a load you could lift only 5 times.

During the six weeks that you are using this daily undulating model, you should feel comfortable with the increasing loads for each set. The Anatomical Adaptation (AA) and SM phases are unchanged.

COMPLEX TRAINING

One of the most effective ways to build muscular power, especially for running and cycling, is plyometrics, a form of exercise involving explosive movements, such as jumping over or onto a high box. Including such exercises in your weekly training routine can be quite effective, although fitting in one more workout may seem impossible. The answer is to combine plyometrics and weights into one session. This is known as "complex training."

Complex training not only saves time but also magnifies the benefit of the plyometrics. This is because lifting weights stimulates the nervous system to activate more muscle fibers for a couple of minutes following an exercise. And activating large numbers of muscle fibers during a plyometrics exercise means greater power generation. Combining the two disciplines into one workout radically improves power.

FIGURE 14: Jump-Up

To do a complex training workout, you simply alternate strength training and plyometrics: After a set of weight lifting, rest for 1 minute and then do one set of 10 to 15 repetitions of a plyometric exercise that involves the same muscle groups in essentially the same movement patterns as the preceding weight exercise. For example, following a set of step-ups, squats, or leg presses, do a set of explosive jump-ups onto a box (Figure 14). Table 5 offers examples of plyometric workouts to pair with weight-lifting exercises.

The quality of training is the key to gaining both strength and power. This means gradually increasing your effort—lifting heavier weights, jumping higher, throwing farther, using heavier implements, and moving with increased speed. By combining weights and plyometrics into a single workout and limiting exercises to the multijoint movements that most closely simulate the movements of swimming, cycling, and running, you can dramatically improve both strength and power.

Training for both strength and power should be considered a long-term process. Generally it takes six weeks to build muscle, so if you decide to do complex training, make the commitment to incorporate it throughout the season. Doing only a couple of weeks of this type of training will do more harm than good. Early on in the season, during the AA period, the exercises involve low weight loads and low-intensity plyometric movements. This is when you are getting the hang of doing the movements that are involved in both types of training and refining them.

TABLE 5: Complex Training Exercise Pairings

STRENGTH EXERCISE	PAIRED PLYOMETRIC EXERCISE
Step-up, Squat, Leg Press	Rope skipping, jumps onto low box, jumps onto high box
Lat Pull-down	Overhead medicine ball throw (increase ball weight or throw distance)
Bench Press, Push-up	Clap push-up (increase reps)
Abdominal	Medicine ball "catch and throw" on decline bench (increase ball weight or throw distance)
Heel Raise	Vertical jump for height

Following AA, as you move into the MT and MS periods, gradually increase both the weight loads and the plyometric intensities. For example, move from rope skipping to low-box jumping to high-box jumping.

The MS period is when you will take on the most challenging exercises and should last about four weeks, with eight to twelve total sessions. The development of strength and power is the primary focus of your training during this period, which coincides with Base 1. After Base 1 you should begin to cut back on both weight training and plyometrics in order to shift the emphasis to swimming, cycling, and running.

Complex training is called "complex" because it involves the combination of two disciplines, but it is also "complicated." There is no simple way of laying out a program that fits everyone. The serious athlete who decides to try complex training will need to experiment—cautiously. Be conservative with the increases you undertake, not only in terms of loads and repetitions with weights but also in regard to the height, weight, distance, and repetitions of the plyometric exercises.

14: Unique Needs

The principle of individualization demands that in order to achieve athletic success, the various training components (volume, workload, intensity, frequency, duration) must match the unique needs and capabilities of the athlete. Although it is not possible to provide specific details for every individual in a book such as this, it is possible to provide general direction for rather homogeneous groups. Five clusters of athletes are examined in this chapter—women, masters, juniors, novices, and elite athletes.

GRAND MASTERS AND SENIORS

In the early days of triathlon, the 55–59 group was the oldest age group recognized in racing. It was rare that anyone over age 60 would even be at the race as a spectator, let alone competing. Now athletes in their sixties, seventies, and even eighties are competing at all distances, from sprint to Ironman, and their numbers are growing every year. Seniors such as Sister Madonna Buder, Harriet Anderson, Bob Scott, and Robert McKeague are role models for thousands of young, aspiring triathletes. They and others like them have taught us that age no longer means what it did a generation ago when the sport was in its infancy.

Everything described in Chapter 14 of the *Training Bible* on masters also applies to grand masters—only more so. Whereas forty-something athletes can still make training mistakes and discover that their bodies will still adapt and forgive them, athletes in their seventies or eighties at some point

TRIATHLETE'S
TRAINING BIBLE
2nd ed.

*See pp. 206–209
for more on
Masters*

103

find out this is no longer the case. The older you are, the fewer mistakes you can make and still get away with it. This means getting the details dialed in exactly right for nutrition, rest and recovery, strength training, volume, intensity, equipment, and everything else that affects health and performance. Errors in judgment at these ages mean unusable joints, surgery, broken bones, and, at the very least, days lost to overwhelming fatigue.

The good news is that athletes who have reached these ages tend to be both patient and wise. They see triathlon as a lifestyle, not as something to be defeated and vanquished. They're in it for the long haul. Younger athletes could learn a lot from them. If science could figure out how to put a grand master's wisdom into the mind of a 25-year-old physical specimen, it would create the ultimate athlete.

> For grand masters and seniors, errors in judgment at these ages mean unusable joints, surgery, broken bones, and, at the very least, days lost to overwhelming fatigue.

How should the grand master and senior athlete train? To remain in top shape and continue racing, they especially need to keep challenging the muscular system. This means including strength training, hill work, and open-water swims in the training program on a regular basis, yet keeping such workouts widely spaced to allow time for recovery. It is especially important for them to continue their strength training program, as this will benefit not only their triathlon performance but also the quality of their lives in general. Research with 90-year-olds has found that their rate of improvement in strength is the same as that of 20-year-olds when they are put on a similar resistance training program.

Grand masters and senior athletes have well-honed swimming, cycling, and running skills; if they do not, the risk of injury is greatly magnified. It is never too late to learn good skills—focus on technique, if necessary, to reduce that risk, if you are a masters or grand masters athlete. In nutrition, you must emphasize alkaline-enhancing foods in the vegetable and fruit categories to minimize acidic body fluids and the loss of muscle and bone. See Chapter 16 of the *Training Bible* for more details.

TRIATHLETE'S
TRAINING BIBLE
2nd ed.

See p. 251,
Table 16.4

15: The Training Diary

A training diary is especially helpful to the self-coached, time-constrained triathlete or duathlete who must make every hour of training count. It's also a source of information about what has or hasn't worked in the past, the progress you are making, the need for recovery, how your body responds to a given workout, and how much recovery is necessary following breakthrough workouts and races.

TRIATHLETE'S
TRAINING BIBLE
2nd ed.

See pp. 234–236
for more on
Using a Diary
for Analysis

A diary is not an end in itself. If you write down workouts, but never use the data, the diary's full potential to help you achieve peak racing fitness is not realized.

TRAINING ANALYSIS SOFTWARE

Chances are good that you have some experience with computer software as a tool to help you analyze the data you download from devices such as power meters, heart rate monitors, GPS devices, and accelerometers. The manufacturers of training equipment nearly always include such software with the purchase of the device. Some of these are quite basic but others are fairly complex.

The problem with most software that comes in the box with a new device is that it was designed by a company that may make excellent hardware but knows little about software. Unfortunately, the manufacturer also does not usually know what's important in training. Training analysis software designed by knowledgeable athletes in a software-focused company is usually better than what came in the box.

One of the best software analysis tools is called "WKO+" and is available online at TrainingPeaks.com. I admit I'm rather partial, as I've played a small role in its development and use it to analyze all of my clients' training and racing data. It's a powerful tool for the serious athlete and makes analysis simple for almost any training device you own. It's great for analyzing heart rate, power, and pacing data regardless of your device's manufacturer.

> **If your software doesn't help you easily determine whether you are improving, then it is useless.**

No matter what software you use, the key question you want answered has to do with your progress toward race goals—"Am I improving?" If the software doesn't help you figure this out easily, then it is useless. The software should be capable of performing several key functions:

- It should be able to track your time in each heart rate, power, and pace zone by workout and for the entire season.
- It should allow you to change your zones, especially in power and pacing, as your fitness changes.
- It should provide a way for you to quickly compare similar workouts.
- You should be able to record changes in pace or power relative to body weight.
- There should be an easy way to track improvements in workout pace or power for similar workouts.
- You should be able to track your capacity for handling greater training stress.
- It should be possible for you to use the data to gauge the level of fatigue you can manage without breaking down.
- A graphic or metric should be provided that shows how your fitness is progressing.
- There should be a way to determine when you are ready to race.

Even if you decide to use software to help you interpret your training data, it can still be incredibly useful to keep a diary. If the hard-copy approach provided in the *Training Bible* doesn't work for you, there are plenty of electronic formats that might suit you better. Regardless, a diary helps you see the big picture by keeping all the details in focus, both the hard data and the subjective feedback. When used effectively, it serves as an excellent tool for planning your steps, motivating you, and diagnosing your problems. It also provides a personal history of training and racing accomplishments. A well-kept diary ranks right up there with training, rest, and nutrition when it comes to developing a competitive edge.

16: Fuel

How and what should you eat to maximize performance now and for many healthy years to come? The possibilities are nearly endless—and endlessly confusing. In this chapter I discuss the triathlete's nutritional needs and how to meet those needs.

BODY WEIGHT MANAGEMENT

It's been my experience that many triathletes want to know how to lose weight to improve climbing on the bike and running in general. There's little doubt that being lighter means climbing and running faster. A pound of excess body weight takes about 2 watts to get up a hill on a bike and costs about 2 seconds a mile when running. So dropping 10 pounds of excess flab means you'll ride up a hill 7 to 10 percent faster and run a 5 km about a minute faster than you do now. Those are significant improvements in performance that would otherwise take months of hard training to accomplish.

This is not to say that all triathletes should lose weight. Many are already lean enough, but how can you tell if you're in the correct range? You really can't base your evaluation just on weight—200 pounds may sound heavy, but if a 200-pound athlete was 7 feet tall, he would be very skinny. A better way to think about your body weight is to compare it with height. Determine your weight-to-height ratio by dividing your weight in pounds by your height in inches. Competitive male triathletes are generally about 2.1 to 2.3 pounds per inch. High-performance women triathletes are usually about 1.8 to 2.0.

If your ratio is above this range, how can you get it closer to the "ideal?" Unfortunately, there have been few studies of serious athletes that looked at this question. One group of researchers, however, has examined the issue in an interesting way. They compared eating less with exercising more to see which was more effective in helping athletes drop excess body fat.

The scientists had six endurance-trained men create a 1,000-calorie-per-day deficit for seven days by either exercising more while maintaining their caloric intake or eating less while keeping exercise the same. With 1,000 calories of increased exercise daily—comparable to running an additional 8 miles or so each day—the men averaged 1.67 pounds of weight loss in a week. The subjects eating 1,000 fewer calories each day lost 4.75 pounds on average for the week.

So, according to this study, the old adage that "a calorie is a calorie" doesn't hold true. At least in the short term, restricting food intake appears to have a greater return *on the scales* than increasing training workload does.

Notice that I said "on the scales." The reduced-food-intake group in this study unfortunately lost a greater percentage of muscle mass than the increased-exercise group did. That is an ineffective way to lose weight. If the scales show you're lighter, but you have less muscle to create power, the trade-off is not a good one.

How can you reduce calories and yet maintain muscle mass? Unfortunately, that question hasn't been answered for athletes. One study did address it for sedentary women, however, and the conclusions may be applicable to athletes.

In 1994, Italian researchers had 25 women eat only 800 calories a day for 21 days. Ten ate a relatively high-protein, low-carbohydrate diet. Fifteen ate a low-protein, high-carbohydrate diet. Both groups were restricted to 20 percent of calories from fat. The two groups lost similar amounts of weight, but there was a significantly greater loss of muscle for the women on the high-carbohydrate, low-protein diet.

So if cutting calories is a more effective way to lose weight than increasing training workload, it appears that the protein content of the diet must be kept at near-normal levels. This assumes that you're eating adequate protein before starting the diet, which many athletes aren't. If your protein intake is already low, typically less than about 20 percent of total calories, then dieting will negatively affect training quality and you are likely to lose muscle mass.

It seems that when you are trying to lose those last few pounds of excess fat, cutting calories is more effective than increasing exercise volume. But a quality source of protein should be included in every meal. The best time in the season to lose weight is during the Base period. The closer you get to your A-priority race, the more detrimental calorie-cutting will be to your recovery and performance.

THE FIVE STAGES OF RECOVERY

In Chapter 16 of the Training Bible I explained periodization as it relates to your diet—that is, varying the mix of foods throughout the year in order to best meet your training needs. The stages of recovery put this principle into practice to help you recover faster after each workout.

TRIATHLETE'S TRAINING BIBLE 2nd ed.

See pp. 250–251 for more on Periodization of Diet

In the Paleo diet, which is discussed in this chapter, it may sound as if carbohydrates are the "bad guy" in an endurance athlete's diet. On the contrary, eating carbohydrates is necessary for high levels of performance. But the timing of carbohydrate intake is critical to success. In fact, if your carb intake is timed correctly, you can actually cut back a bit on the amount and take in a wider variety of nutrient-dense foods. Those foods can in turn help you recover faster and perform at a higher level.

The key is to accept that your workouts are the central events of each day, and that the types of foods you eat are determined by when those workouts take place. This is likely a fairly easy notion to acquire, since, as a serious athlete, you probably already have a "training is life, everything else is just the details" way of seeing the world.

The key is to accept that your workouts are the central events of each day, and that the types of foods you eat are determined by when those workouts take place.

Each workout has five feeding times linked with it. I call these "stages." Here's how they work.

Stage 1: Before the Workout

The goal of this stage is to store sufficient carbohydrate to get you through the workout. This is especially important for early-morning sessions. For the perfect fuel, eat 200 to 400 calories, primarily from a moderate-glycemic-index, carbohydrate-rich food, two hours before the workout. Of course, few are willing to get up at 3 a.m. just to eat before a 5 a.m. masters swim session. Instead, take a bottle of your favorite sports drink or a couple of gel packets with 12 ounces of water to the workout. Ten minutes before the warm-up begins, start taking in your "breakfast." This isn't quite as good as eating a real breakfast two hours beforehand, but it's far better than training on a low fuel tank.

2 Hours Before the Workout				
Calories	Source	Glycemic Index		
		low	med	high
200–400	carbohydrates		×	

Stage 2: During the Workout

For an hour or less of training, water is all you need, assuming you refilled the tank in Stage 1. For longer workouts you also need carbohydrates, and the amount of carbohydrates you should take in increases with the length of the workout. It could be as little as 120 calories or as much as 500 calories of carbs per hour, depending not only on workout length but also on body size, workout intensity, and your personal experience.

These carbohydrates should be mostly in the form of liquids from a high-glycemic-index source. The best choice is your favorite sports drink. You could also use gels, chased immediately by lots of water. The longer the workout, the more important the carbohydrates are for top performance and good recovery later. It's usually a good idea for a liquid fuel source to include sodium, especially if it's hot and you sweat heavily. The research is less than overwhelming on the benefits of other ingredients, including potassium, magnesium, and protein. Include them if you want to. If you pay careful attention as you train and experiment with your nutrition, you can develop a sense of the type of carbohydrate that works best for you and the amount you need for different workouts.

For Longer Workouts				
Calories	Source	Glycemic Index		
		low	med	high
120–500/hour	carbohydrates (with sodium)			×

Stage 3: Immediately After the Workout

This and the next stage are the key times in the day for taking in carbohydrates. When athletes say that eating in stages leaves them hungry or fatigued, it's nearly always because they don't take in enough carbohydrates in Stages 3 and 4.

Your goal now is to replace the carbohydrate used during the workout. In the first 30 minutes or so after a workout, your body is several hundred times more sensitive to carbohydrate and will readily store more than at any other time of the day. The longer you wait to refuel, the less likely you are to completely refill the gas tank. Take in three to four calories per pound of body weight, mostly from high-glycemic-index carbohydrates, in this stage.

You can buy a commercial product for this type of refueling, but they are expensive. You can make your own recovery drink by blending the following ingredients:

Combine 16 ounces of fruit juice with:

1 banana

3–5 tbsp. glucose (such as Carbo-Pro, available at sportquestdirect.com), depending on body size

2–3 tbsp. protein powder (egg or whey sources are best)

2–3 pinches of salt

Consuming this drink during the 30-minute, post-workout window is critical for recovery. It should be your highest priority after a hard workout. If the workout lasted less than an hour and was low-intensity, omit this stage.

Immediately After High-Intensity or Long Workouts				
Calories	Source	Glycemic Index		
		low	med	high
3–4/lb. body weight	carbohydrates			×

Stage 4: As Long as the Workout Lasted

Continue to focus your diet on carbohydrates, especially from moderate- to high-glycemic-index sources, for a time period equal to the amount of time you were working out. Take in some protein as well. You may be ready to eat a meal in Stage 4 if the workout was long. Now is the time to eat starches such as pasta, bread, bagels, cereal, rice, corn, and other foods rich in fast-absorbing glucose to facilitate the recovery process. Perhaps the perfect foods to eat at this time are potatoes, sweet potatoes, yams, and bananas, since they also have a net alkaline-enhancing quality that reduces body acidity following workouts. Raisins are a great snack food for Stage 4. Eat until satisfied. If you feel full after only a small meal, try eating several smaller meals during this period.

Post-Workout (for as long as the workout lasted)				
Calories	Source		Glycemic Index	
		low	med	high
As needed	carbohydrates, protein		×	×

Stage 5: Until the Next Workout

Usually, by the time Stage 5 comes around, you will be at work, back in class, spending time with your family, mowing the grass, or doing whatever it is you do when not training or racing. Although this part of your day may look ordinary to the rest of the world, it really isn't. You can still focus on nutrition for long-term recovery.

This is the time when many athletes get sloppy with their diets. The most common mistake is to continue to eat Stage 3 and 4 foods that are low in nutrient value and high in starch and sugar. Such foods are great for immediate recovery but not effective for building up long-term nutritional stores. The most nutrient-dense foods are vegetables, fruits, and lean protein from animal sources, especially seafood. Snack on nuts, seeds, and berries. All of these foods are rich in vitamins, minerals, and other trace elements necessary for health, growth, and recovery.

Avoid processed foods that come in packages, including those with labels that say "healthy." They aren't, and that even includes foods invented by sports nutrition scientists. They are still several million years behind nature in producing nutritious chow. Just eat *real* food in Stage 5.

If you are doing two or three workouts in a day, you may not get to Stage 5 until late in the day. Also, Stage 4 may replace Stage 1 with closely spaced workouts. That's not a problem.

That's all there is to it—a simple way of organizing your day into five stages of eating to ensure adequate recovery and optimal health. You can find more details on this topic in my book *The Paleo Diet for Athletes.*

Pareto and Perfection

Vilfredo Pareto was an Italian economist of the late nineteenth and early twentieth centuries who discovered that 80 percent of the land in Italy was owned by 20 percent of the population. Experts in other fields soon discovered that this "80-20 Rule" also applied to their areas of study. For example, 80 percent of the productivity in a business is typically generated by 20 percent of the employees. Schoolchildren spend 80 percent of their time with 20 percent of their friends. Investors find that 80 percent of their income comes from 20 percent of their stock. The 80-20 Rule is also known as the "Pareto Principle."

His rule also applies to your diet. The Pareto Principle says that you don't need to eat perfectly. Stage 5 of recovery is often viewed as being quite restrictive, since your diet must be focused on fruits, vegetables, and lean protein. The 80-20 Rule tells us that it's okay to occasionally eat a cookie, a slice of pizza, a piece of bread, or even a bit of pasta in Stage 5—so long as this makes up less than 20 percent of your food intake. In other words, it's perfectly acceptable to cheat a little. Just make sure that 80 percent of the calories on your plate is nutrient-dense, and you will be healthy, lean, fit, and fast. You can thank Vilfredo for that.

About the Author

Joe Friel is the founder and president of Training Bible Coaching, with endurance coaches around the world who learn and apply the coaching philosophy and methods described in this book. Training Bible Coaching's athletes include recreational and elite triathletes, duathletes, cyclists, mountain bikers, runners, and swimmers.

Joe has an extensive background in coaching, having trained endurance athletes since 1980. His clients have included novices, elite amateurs, and professionals. The list includes an Ironman Triathlon winner, USA and foreign national champions, world championship competitors, and an Olympian.

As well as *The Triathlete's Training Bible*, Joe is the author of *The Cyclist's Training Bible*, *Cycling Past 50*, *Precision Heart Rate Training* (co-author), *The Mountain Biker's Training Bible*, *Going Long: Training for Training for Triathlon's Ultimate Challenge* (co-author), *The Paleo Diet for Athletes* (co-author), *Your First Triathlon*, and *Total Heart Rate Training*. He is the editor of the VeloPress series Ultrafit Multisport Training. He holds a master's degree in exercise science and is a USA Triathlon and USA Cycling–certified elite coach. He helped to found the USA Triathlon National Coaching Commission and served two terms as chair.

Joe is also a columnist for *Inside Triathlon* and *VeloNews* magazines and writes feature stories for other international magazines and websites. His opinions on matters related to training for endurance sports are widely sought and have been featured in such publications as *Runner's World*, *Outside*, *Triathlete*, *220*, *Women's Sports & Fitness*, *Men's Fitness*, *American Health*, *Masters Sports*, *Walking*, *Bicycling*, the *New York Times*, and even *Vogue*.

He conducts yearly seminars and camps on training and racing for endurance athletes and provides consulting services to corporations in the fitness industry and to national governing bodies.

As an age-group competitor, he is a former Colorado State Masters Triathlon Champion and a Rocky Mountain region and Southwest region duathlon age-group champion, has been named to several All-American teams, and has represented the United States at the world championships. He also competes in USA Cycling bike races.

Joe Friel may be contacted through his website at trainingbible.com.